Praise for Monday Morning Choices by David Cottrell

"Are your choices moving you toward success or away from it? This upbeat book will leave you feeling passionate about choosing a positive future for yourself!" —Ken Blanchard, author of *The One Minute Manager* and *Know Can Do!*

"*Monday Morning Choices* gives sound, insightful direction to anyone wanting to get off the wrong track and onto the road to success, both professionally and personally. Interesting, easy to read and highly engaging." —Stephen R. Covey, author of *The 8th Habit: From Effectiveness to Greatness*

"*Monday Morning Choices* is a terrific handbook for improving your game as a leader. The advice and stories are simple and profound." —Noel M. Tichy, coauthor of *Judgment: How Winning Leaders Make Great Calls*

"*Monday Morning Choices* is a great reference for anybody who is committed to taking their game to the next level." —Kevin Sabin, President and Chief Operating Officer, Arvest Bank Group

"The wind and the rain or storms of life do not determine our destiny. Neither do other people and their opinions determine our future. What does affect our lives is our power to choose. Choose to read this fine work." —James H. Amos Jr., Chairman and CEO, Tasti D' Lite

"All David wants you to do is make a choice. Once a week. It only takes a few minutes. The first choice you can make is in reading this book. I hope you do." —Seth Godin, author of *The Dip*

"David Cottrell is one of the finest authors I know anything about. His newest book, *Monday Morning Choices* will help you achieve extraordinary levels of performance. So goes Monday, so goes the week." —Garry Kinder, The KBI Group

Monday Morning
Choices

Also by David Cottrell

www.CornerStoneLeadership.com

CHANGE YOUR MONDAY
AND CHANGE YOUR LIFE!

Monday Morning
Choices

12 Powerful Ways
to Go from Everyday
to Extraordinary

David Cottrell

Collins
An Imprint of HarperCollinsPublishers

To every brave individual who has the courage
to make tough decisions that will change his or
her life.

HarperCollins books may be purchased for educational, business, or sales promotional use. For information, please write: Special Markets Department, HarperCollins Publishers, 10 East 53rd Street, New York, NY 10022.

FIRST EDITION

Designed by Sarah Maya Gubkin

Library of Congress Cataloging-in-Publication Data
Cottrell, David, 1953–
Monday morning choices : 12 powerful ways to go from everyday to extraordinary / David Cottrell.
p.   cm.
ISBN 978–0–06–145191–1
1. Choice (Psychology) 2. Success—Psychological aspects. I. Title.
BF611.C68 2007
158—dc22
2007024755
08 09 10 11 12   ID/RRD   10 9 8 7 6 5 4 3

Monday Morning
Choices

Change Your Mondays and Change Your Life

Monday, Monday, so good to me...
LYRICS FROM "MONDAY, MONDAY"
BY THE MAMAS AND THE PAPAS

Each of us has a different idea of success. Whether you strive for money, power, happiness, love, or anything else, your choices will determine whether you reach your goals. How to make the right choices, even when they're hard, is what *Monday Morning Choices* is all about.

What if you could begin changing your life by simply investing twenty minutes every Monday morning for twelve weeks?

I am not talking about spending twenty minutes every

Monday scratching off lotto tickets and hoping your luck and your life will change. Of course, we all wish success were that easy. It's not!

But, here's the good news: you have control over your life and your success on the basis of the choices you make. This book will outline a plan for you to invest twenty minutes every Monday focusing on one personal and positive choice you will make during that week. I promise: you will change your life.

Why Monday? Why not Tuesday or Friday or any other day? I think that Monday sets the tone for the rest of your week. I have found that most people dread starting a new week, but I love Mondays! It's the one day of the week when I can get a head start on everybody else, simply because I choose to embrace Monday morning.

We spend the majority of our time at work. What we do at work has a ripple effect through the rest of our lives. If, each Monday morning, you make a choice to move into the new work week with renewed commitment and passion, you can change all areas of your life. You can truly change your Mondays and change your life!

Monday Morning Choices is about focusing on twelve timeless and proven principles for successful living. You can experience success and happiness by integrating these choices into all areas of your life.

How Can You Be More Successful Right Now?

If you ask that question of ten people in a typical organization, many will say they believe that success is a matter of being in the right place at the right time. Some will say that successful people are just lucky—good fortune falls into their laps. Some may even attribute success to their ancestors or their genes—they inherited a position of success. No matter how you define success, you create it by making better choices.

Has anyone ever been entirely successful because of good luck?

Maybe, but not likely! Some may have succeeded because of luck, but you surely can't rely on luck to get you where you want to be.

Luck, happenstance, being in the right place at the right time, and family inheritance all may help, of course, but the reality is this: many people may be in the right place at the right time, may have had good fortune come their way, or were born into a wealthy family; yet, they've never experienced success. Others face nothing but adversity their whole lives, but they manage to wind up on top.

Take a look at the successful people you know in your office, your neighborhood, your city, or your family. Without exception, their success has been created by their choices.

It's not about luck, the conditions, or even the guardian angels guiding their lives.

These successful people share some common traits,

but—believe it or not—there is not an enormous difference between highly successful people and those who are not so successful.

For instance, do you think the salesperson who earns $250,000 a year has five times the intellect or the ability of the salesperson earning $50,000 a year selling the same product in a similar territory? Does the $250,000-a-year salesperson work five times as hard?

Of course not!

Most people are within 10 percent of the same IQ. Most people work about the same number of hours, the same number of days per week. So what's the difference? Successful people make choices others don't like to make—and by doing things differently, they make choices that improve their success.

Successful people have just as hard a time making difficult choices as everyone else. The difference is that they persevere. They realize there is often great reward for those difficult choices. Their personal goals and professional goals are so vivid in their minds that they realize the result they will accomplish is well worth the price of a difficult choice.

Regardless of how you personally define it, success is ultimately realized by people who make more good choices and recover quickly from their bad choices. Our personal and professional success depends on repeating good choices, day in and day out, and avoiding repetition of bad choices.

So how do you go about making those difficult choices?

Types of Choices

Most choices that help create success are never recognized by others. They are **personal choices** people make that mold their character. These character choices are internal choices known only to the person making them. Those choices include accepting responsibility, commitment, values, and integrity. Those are personal choices that we make deep within ourselves and that eventually mold our life.

There are **action choices** that will lead you toward success. Those choices help you move beyond simply talking the talk and toward getting things done. These choices are the catalyst for moving forward; they lubricate the process of getting things done. They include the choices of sticking to the objective long enough to win, being enthusiastic about work and life, and attacking and conquering difficult issues.

Then, there are **investment choices**. I'm not referring to the stock market or a get-rich-quick scheme. The important investment choices are about investing in people who will make your life better. You cannot be successful in the long term without investing in relationships, accepting constructive criticism, seeking the truth, and giving back to others.

This book, based on the experiences of many and the observations of many more, will provide insight into twelve choices others have made—and you can make—to enhance your success in your career and in your life.

The path we'll mark is not an easy one to follow. The best

choices are rarely the easiest. However, the sum total of these twelve choices creates a philosophy that allows you to make better decisions while encouraging success in every aspect of your life.

The Challenge

Making good choices is a never-ending challenge. It requires hard work and daily diligence. Life requires that we choose between alternatives every hour of the day, every day of our lives. Making good choices requires constant focus and attention.

Bad choices that seemed so right at the time sometimes turn out to be major impediments to our lives. Want proof? Just read the divorce statistics for your community, or, as you drive to work notice the businesses that have closed.

Our daily challenge is to live our character, action, and investment choices so naturally that we begin making the best choices almost subconsciously. This requires patience, honest reflection, adaptation, and commitment.

The Privilege of Choosing

Making choices is a privilege, one that gives us a freedom we should never take for granted.

A graduate researcher, after a week of following an inmate's schedule from dawn to dusk each day at a state penitentiary, reported that the most difficult part of prison life and incarceration was its lack of choices. "Inmates are denied choices over when life happens, from when to arise each day to when to shower, exercise, work, eat, or retire," she said. "It was one of the most traumatic experiences of my life."

Isn't it interesting? In our free and democratic society, punishment comes in the form of reducing people's ability to make even the most basic choices in their everyday lives. Those inmates will confirm that life without choices is no way to live. Our choices are our privilege! Life is filled with pressures that force us to make constant and immediate choices. Yet, as the prison researcher found, a life without choices is not a good way to live.

Think it's too late to embrace a new philosophy? Or maybe you're worried that you can't make the right choices? It is never too late! According to psychologist Abraham Maslow, "The story of the human race is the story of men and women selling themselves short."

Don't sell yourself short. You can make better choices beginning today to achieve what you want in life tomorrow.

The Game Plan to Change Your Mondays and Change Your Life

- Find at least five people at your office who will join you on your Change Your Mondays—Change Your Life journey. Find people who want to move forward and are willing to pay a small price (about one hour a week—forty minutes of preliminary reading and twenty minutes of meeting every Monday morning) to improve their life.

- Make sure everyone has a *Monday Morning Choices* book. During the week, each of you should read the chapter that will be discussed the following Monday. It will be even more effective if you read the chapter at home with a partner and discuss it before you talk about it with your team at work.

- Arrive at work twenty minutes early for the next twelve Mondays prepared to discuss the choices revealed in the chapter of the week.

- Make a commitment to do something different, based on the chapter your group is discussing.

- Begin changing your Mondays and changing your life!

Of course, you could do this by yourself, but I strongly recommend that you invite others to make the journey with you. It is easier to make changes when you are supporting one another along the way, but more important, you will be teaching, sharing, and investing in other people.

You will receive far more in return than you invest.

During the twelve weeks you will need to encourage one another to commit to move forward. One of the greatest gifts you can give is encouragement, and your inspiration will fill others with renewed courage, spirit, and hope.

Seize the power that choices offer. With good choices, you will take control of your success.

It is up to you. Change Your Mondays and you can Change Your Life!

I hope you will choose to read on, learn, make the right choices, encourage others, and become the successful person you want to be.

Part I

Character Choices: The Foundation of Success

Character is the foundation upon which one must build to win respect. Just as no worthy building can be erected on a weak foundation, so no lasting reputation worthy of respect can be built on a weak character.

R.C. SAMSEL

Monday Morning Choice #1

The No-Victim Choice
. . . Don't Let Your Past
Eat Your Future

Never be bullied into silence. Never allow yourself to be made a victim.
Accept no one's definition of your life, but define yourself.
HARVEY S. FIRESTONE

Poor Gary.

That's what they call him: "Poor Gary." He labors all day in that tiny rear cubicle. His co-workers feel sorry for Gary because he seems to have all the bad luck. He works with the worst territories, the poorest accounts, and the most impossible schedules. Just when he thinks he's closed the deal that will put him over quota, the bottom drops out, and at the end of the month his numbers fall short of the standard.

As the next month begins, Poor Gary's shoulders are more stooped, his head more bowed, and his expression more defeated. His performance lags further behind expectation, and his sales calls are lackluster. Think Poor Gary's results will improve this month? Not likely.

A victim is a person to whom life happens. Without question, Poor Gary falls into the victim category. However, Gary's woes could be caused by his choice to be a victim. He complains about bad management, bad luck, being in a bad situation. Gary is a victim of all the bad things that happen to him.

At the other end of the hall in the same organization is Colin Myers. Colin began in the same small cubicle and worked the territory Gary now occupies. The difference between Colin and Gary is that Gary chooses to be a victim, while Colin made the no-victim choice.

Whenever the unexpected, bad luck, and bad situations occurred, Colin chose to dig deeper to make good things happen. When an order didn't come through, Colin spent time evaluating why he did not get the order, and he made adjustments to help his next call be successful.

In other words, Colin didn't wait for life to happen to him. He made choices to make things happen that would move him forward.

Colin's performance resulted in several promotions, which moved him from the tiny rear cubicle where he had started into the manager's office. From his point of view, the sky remains the limit. Colin had the ability to deal with what-ever came his way, and good things kept coming his way.

Meanwhile, Gary was the perpetual victim of bad luck. Coincidence? Probably not.

Drivers or Passengers

On any of life's journeys, we have to make a choice before we begin the trip. Our options are these: we can be a passenger, or we can be the driver. It's our choice.

People who choose to be passengers are subject to going where other drivers are going. Passengers have no control over the speed with which they move ahead, nor do they have any say about whether or not rules are observed.

Then again, being a passenger is appealing. Passengers merely sit in the car, relaxed and oblivious to their final des-tination. They may put on headphones and listen to music, or they may nap. They may talk on the cell phone or do crossword puzzles. However, they rarely pay attention to where they are, who is in front of them or behind them, or whether progress is being made. Their journey may be pleas-ant enough, but those choosing to be passengers are just going along for the ride.

Those who choose to be drivers accept responsibility for moving forward toward their goals. They pay attention and focus on getting to their final destination. They make deci-sions about how quickly they move ahead. They avoid ob-stacles, like bumps or dips in the road. They may choose to take a detour. They decide when to stop and refuel. During the journey they make the choices to control their safety and success.

The distance between a passenger and a driver in a car is less than three feet, but the difference is huge. The driver has the choice to head toward success. The passenger just goes where he is driven.

In the previous example, Colin was a driver. Gary was a passenger.

Which would you rather be: driver or passenger? The choice is yours.

Responding to the Unexpected

Many people choose to be a victim because something unexpected happens—something completely out of their control. Others have an uncanny ability to deal successfully with the unexpected, the unusual, and the extraordinary. Positively dealing with the unexpected by looking for solutions, not excuses, is the choice you need to make.

If you know someone who is masterful at dealing with the unexpected, take a closer look at that individual, because you've truly met a special person.

Jim Lawton was like that—he was a driver. Whatever came his way, Jim could handle. His dad died while Jim was a freshman in college, and as tuition money dwindled Jim found enough work to support himself and pay his tuition so he could continue his college education.

After graduating, Jim went to work for a company that eventually had to downsize. When that happened, Jim networked his way into a new company and a new job. Notice I didn't say "a better job." No, Jim found an ordinary job and mined each opportunity to move ahead. Jim hasn't allowed anything to keep him from being successful, no matter what life has tossed his way.

Jim chooses to avoid becoming a victim of life's circumstances. He made up his mind to deal with the unexpected. Jim knew that there was no "grand conspiracy" preventing life from being easy for him. Jim also knew it was not what happened to him but rather his response to what happened that would make the difference. Today, Jim is successfully accomplishing his personal and professional goals.

Let me repeat Jim's lesson—it's not what happens to us but how we choose to respond to what happens that determines our next move, next path, next relationship, and next risk.

Believe it or not, the unexpected is going to happen. It's your choice how you deal with it. You can be a victim, or you can choose to realize that by taking control of the unexpected, you can make strides toward greater success.

Do we occasionally fall into the victim trap? Of course. Occasionally feeling like a victim is natural, but remaining in the victim trap will prevent you from achieving success.

Avoiding the victim trap is not easy, but it's a choice you have to make. You control your next move. Will you sit and sulk, or will you commit to continuing toward your ultimate goal?

Victims, Victims, Excuses, Excuses

When did this epidemic of victimization begin? Maybe it has become too easy for people to blame their mistakes on outside circumstances. It's the easy way out, but it's never the best.

Follow the proceedings of any criminal trial, and you will witness some incredible defenses:

- He was caught with the murder weapon, but he was abused as a child.

- Her shoplifting was witnessed by several people, but she's the product of a broken home.

- He did it, but he has untreated attention deficit hyperactive syndrome.

- Her mother didn't love her.

- He grew up in a rough neighborhood.

- He was bullied in school.

Victims, victims everywhere!
In business, it's much the same:

"My department has been hit with turnover, so we didn't meet our deadline."

"We just can't find people who want to work."

These victims are full of excuses, excuses, excuses. Whatever happened to "The Buck Stops Here"?

Being a victim and making excuses rather than the no-victim choice will eventually destroy you. Accept responsibility, and people will recognize your maturity and calm in difficult situations. They will trust your ability to do a good job under difficult circumstances, and more and better opportunities will come your way!

Move Forward, No Matter What

Once you choose to become a driver and proactively deal with the unexpected, take responsibility and move forward when unfair things come your way. Didn't accomplish your objectives for last month? You have two choices—you can either take responsibility and decide you'll work twice as smart this month to make your goals, or you can wonder "Why me?" and quickly find someone else to blame.

Without fail, when you embrace this "why me" attitude, the victim mentality will paralyze your attitude and your enthusiasm. Left to fester, this paralysis will prevent you from doing what you need to do next.

Instead, you should move into the driver's seat. Confront the victim mentality and say, "Bring it on! I will not become a victim of things beyond my control!" It's your choice.

Not Everything Bad That Happens Is Our Doing

Dr. David Cook, a popular sports psychologist for several professional golfers, says that at least three things happen in a round of golf that are unfair or are not deserved. For example:

1. You hit the ball three hundred yards down the middle of the fairway, and it lands in a divot that should have been repaired.

2. You hit a perfect approach shot to the green and the wind gusts right as the ball approaches, knocking the ball into the sand trap. There was not even a breeze when you struck the ball, and now your ball is buried in the bunker.

3. You hit the perfect putt that goes off line when it hits a bump on the green because someone else forgot to fix his or her ball mark.

The choices available are these: either a golfer complains about the unfair circumstances that led his ball astray, or he accepts the situation and plans his next move. He did not cause the situation, but now he must deal with the result.

Dr. Cook says that the difference between the great golfers and the ones who are in the middle of the pack is how they deal with the things that happen to them. The talent level of professional golfers is not significantly different. It's the ability to move beyond the unfair and unexpected that determines who wins the tournament.

In life, as in golf, not everything bad is our doing. But when bad things happen—things we do not deserve—the next move is ours. We cannot blame the situation and adopt the victim mentality. We must accept the unexpected, take responsibility, and move forward.

Taking Ownership

The good news is this: we can make the choice to avoid becoming victims and get on the road to success. There are no limits to the alternatives you have unless you set them yourself.

A source of stress among most people is the feeling of being out of control. Accepting responsibility, becoming a driver, and making the no-victim choice allows us to take control and move forward. Placing blame only adds to our stress because it puts someone else in control of the problem.

The late Thomas J. Watson, the brilliant man who founded IBM, pushed his leadership personnel toward the resiliency of stumbling five times and getting up six. He flatly wouldn't tolerate the paralysis of becoming a victim.

"If you solve it wrong, it will come back and slap you in the face," Watson said. "Then you can solve it right. Lying dead in the water and doing nothing is comfortable because it is without risk, but it is an absolutely fatal way to manage."

In every situation, whether in your work life or in your personal life, there are always alternatives. You must choose to see them. The challenge is taking off the blinders of victimization and searching for the alternatives to help you reach your potential and achieve the success you deserve.

The key to accepting responsibility—no matter what—is to take ownership of your mind, thoughts, actions, and reactions. Only you can accept this ownership—and, once accepted, it is yours to keep.

Conversely, you cannot give away this ownership by blaming others when things go wrong. But if you have ownership you can direct your thoughts and create your own future, even in the face of adversity, a wrecked project, or a mangled relationship.

No one can make you a victim without your consent. No one!

Do not allow yourself to dwell on unfair things that happen to you. Move forward. As a wise man once told me, "Don't let your past eat your future."

Three Things You Can Do to Make the No-Victim Choice

1. Expect the unexpected. Things beyond your control will happen. How you respond to the unexpected events that come your way is how you regain control.

2. Look for alternatives. There are always alternatives if you choose to look for them. Don't

become paralyzed by falling into the victim trap.

3. Spend your energy searching for solutions, not excuses. No matter what happens, keep moving—one foot in front of the other—toward your personal and professional goals.

Monday Morning Discussion Questions

1. Why is it so easy to fall into the victim mentality?

2. When have we been victimized in the past, and how did we respond?

3. Is it really possible to accept total responsibility for things that happen to us? Does the buck really stop with us?

Words of Wisdom about the No-Victim Choice

Things turn out best for the people who make the best of the way things turn out.

JOHN WOODEN

We are free up to the point of choice, then the choice controls the chooser.

MARY CROWLEY

Life's rewards go to those who let their actions rise above their excuses.

LEE J. COLAN

Destiny is not a matter of chance, it is a matter of choice; it is not a thing to be waited for, it is a thing to be achieved.

WILLIAM JENNINGS BRYAN

The greatest power that a person possesses is the power to choose.

J. MARTIN KOHE

I used to say, "I sure hope things will change." Then I learned that the only way things are going to change for me is when I change.

JIM ROHN

People are always blaming their circumstances for what they are. The people who get on in this world are they who get up and look for the circumstances they want, and, if they can't find them, make them.

GEORGE BERNARD SHAW

One's philosophy is not best expressed in words; it's expressed in the choices one makes. In the long run we shape our lives and we shape ourselves. The process never ends until we die. And the choices we make are ultimately our responsibility.

ELEANOR ROOSEVELT

Life will be to a large extent what we ourselves make of it.

SAMUEL SMILES

Monday Morning Choice #2

The Commitment Choice ... Be Passionate Enough to Succeed

When work, commitment, and pleasure all become one,
and you reach that deep well where passion lives, nothing is impossible.
ANONYMOUS

Most of us are familiar with this drill: We set a goal— let's say it's to improve our fitness level. We set up a training program and buy new running shoes. Maybe we ask someone at the gym to give us some pointers.

Now comes the hard part—regular workouts. We'll do cardiovascular endurance training three times a week and weight training twice a week—one day for the upper body and one day for the lower body.

We set out with a calendar of our activities. The first day, we run two miles. Check. The second day, we lift weights. Check.

The third day . . . well, we had to work late that day, so when we got home, it was too dark to run safely.

The fourth day . . . had a dinner appointment right after work. No weight training.

The fifth day . . . "Okay," we say to ourselves. "We've missed two days. We'll just begin again on Monday."

Monday comes, and, well, one of our co-workers is being promoted and transferred to another state, so we can't miss her going-away party.

Pretty soon it's the end of the month, and we've checked off only two days of our training schedule. "Time flies," we mutter as we flip the calendar to the next month.

So what happened? Apparently, our commitment to improving our fitness wasn't as important as we thought. We were interested but not committed.

Commitment Requires Passion

Commitment isn't as simple as being able to check off what we've accomplished toward our goal. It's a choice, an attitude. It is believing that what we are doing is important enough to stay the course.

People who are successful are passionate about being successful and are willing to pay the price to achieve that goal, the next level, or whatever it is they want to do. Passionate? About commitment? Absolutely! Positively!

When you make the commitment choice, you understand your mission, know the costs, and will do whatever is necessary to accomplish the mission. If you are totally committed, you'll be willing to run through walls to make it happen!

While working at FedEx I saw firsthand the impact of positive people working toward a common goal. When Fred Smith created FedEx, he surrounded himself with a few committed people. Not many others believed his concept would work—it was a little too far out of the box. The concept was that all packages would fly from their city to a central hub in Memphis, Tennessee, to be sorted and loaded on planes returning to the city of the package's destination. It was the first time that a hub-and-spoke system had been thought of as a way to efficiently deliver packages.

Most people wondered, "Why would you deliver a package from San Francisco to Los Angeles through Memphis?" In fact, one of Smith's professors at Yale gave him a C on the paper he submitted that explained his idea. The investment community considered his concept illogical. Would you invest your money or career in such a radical concept?

Mark Twain once said, "The man with a new idea is a crank until the idea succeeds," and plenty of people called Fred Smith a crank in the early 1970s. But Fred understood his mission and invited some creative and committed people to join him. In April 1973, FedEx became a reality.

You can imagine the excitement that first night of operation! Fourteen FedEx planes in fourteen cities made their first midnight trip to Memphis. The packages were sorted and then reloaded on planes that would take them to their destinations. The entire FedEx team was waiting to count the packages and celebrate their success.

One by one they unloaded the planes. When all the packages were counted, there were twelve packages on the fourteen planes. Two more planes than packages! Obviously, that's not a good business model. How discouraging the first night's results must have been!

Yes, everyone was disappointed, but Fred Smith had created a team of people who understood the long-term mission and were committed to pay the price to make it successful. In fact, when money was tight in the early days, several pilots used their personal credit cards to fuel their planes. Those people were committed—and, as they say, the rest is history.

Tonight, FedEx will sort and deliver millions of packages. Revenues are over $50 billion. More than 300,000 employees are on the payroll, thanks to those first committed employees and the leadership of Fred Smith.

Your situation may not lead to a FedEx success story. However, wherever you are, you can leverage your personal success by increasing your commitment and surrounding yourself with others who make the commitment choice.

Why Commitment Fades

Isn't it interesting how our commitment tends to fade over time?

We have great intentions, but something takes precedence over our time and commitment, and we lose our focus. Often we enthusiastically set our goals, map our journeys, and then make little forward progress. What happened to the enthusiasm we felt as we set our goals and made our plans?

Our dreams were the main motivator when we envisioned ourselves fit, faster, and less flabby. We saw ourselves crossing the finish line, winning the race, and impressing everyone who doubted us. We knew we were the best choice for that next promotion. What happened?

Chances are, we were more interested than committed to reaching those goals. We weren't passionate enough to follow through to the end of the journey.

Commitment Begins with Written Goals

Most people do not write down their goals. They are interested in accomplishing them but not committed to state them clearly. Without writing a specific, clear picture of what they want for themselves, they drift aimlessly through life. Personal commitment begins with a crystal-clear understanding of what you are trying to accomplish. I think the lack of understanding the specifics of what they want to accomplish at work and in life is what prevents people from commitment.

If you want to reach your goal, you have to mentally see the goal and then physically write the goal. Just seeing is not good enough—your goal has to be written in your handwriting. Writing down your goals will clarify what you are trying to accomplish. Writing them down marks the beginning of your commitment to accomplish those goals.

Benjamin Franklin made a list of traits he either wanted to get rid of or wanted to cultivate. Then he graded himself on his progress or regression every day. Not yearly, weekly, or monthly, but every day. His question to himself was, "Did I get closer to accomplishing my goals, or did I lose ground today?"

Franklin chose to be more than interested. He was committed enough to his goals to take the time to measure his progress. He was committed enough to keep his goals in view, working in some way each day to take one step forward. That's passionate commitment!

Ben Franklin's Philosophy Still Applies

Writing down and measuring progress toward your goals is not "old school." It's your first step to accomplishing your dreams.

When my son, Michael, left home for college, he proudly announced that he had set his academic goal for his first semester. I had taught him all his life to be a goal setter, and he knew the importance of mentally creating a goal and then physically doing the necessary things to make the goal happen.

I asked him what his goal was for his first semester at Texas A&M. He would not tell me his goal—he said he had it under control—and I did not press him on the matter. I was not certain what his expectations were for himself. My expectations were that he would be involved, have a good time, adjust to being away from home, and not be on scholastic probation after his first semester.

When the semester was over, his transcript was sent directly to him. He opened it, and his grade point average was 3.8. He opened the envelope in which he had placed the sheet of paper where his goal was written to show me the goal he had set at the beginning of the semester. It was 3.8.

Coincidence? Maybe, but probably not. He was focused on a 3.8. He was more than interested in making it happen; he was committed to pay the price to make it happen. His goal was written everywhere: in his wallet, on his mirror, and everywhere he looked. Every day he measured and graded himself, striving for the 3.8 he would eventually achieve.

One irony of that story? I would have suggested that he set his goal lower for his first semester away at school. After all, he beat my own first-semester grade point average by a huge margin! But he set his own goal and was passionately committed to achieve HIS goal.

Written goals—personally set, continually visualized, and important enough to be worth paying the price for success—have a mysterious way of coming true.

Degrees of Commitment

By surrounding yourself with others who choose commitment and passion, you'll find yourself making more progress.

Why? Because we tend to feed off those with similar goals and commitment levels.

Several years ago, the Great Gadzoni had just completed a challenging and dangerous tightrope walk over Niagara Falls. The wind was howling around the aerialist's ears, and stinging rain pelted him as he inched across the rope.

Met with enthusiastic applause from those waiting on the other side, the Great Gadzoni was wringing the water from his cape when an excited fan approached, urging him to make a return trip but this time pushing a wheelbarrow, which the fan just happened to have with him.

The Great Gadzoni was hesitant, having barely made the first trip across in the high winds and pouring rain. But the spectator insisted. "You can do it—I know you can," he urged.

The Great Gadzoni thought for a moment. "You really believe I can do it?"

The spectator nodded excitedly, "Yes, yes. Definitely. You can do it."

"Okay," said the aerialist, taking the wheelbarrow from the man. "Get in."

Makes one wonder whether the spectator's passion for the feat lost its luster at the last minute when he was asked to commit, to invest in the goal. He was interested but not committed.

But isn't this often where we find ourselves just as we've sketched out the final details of a plan to reach a new goal?

The missing ingredient is the choice to commit ourselves, to go where no man or woman has gone before, and, along the way, to endure what no one else would want to endure in order to discover success we have never known.

How Powerful Are You?

Do you find yourself on the brink of a commitment, and you just can't take the leap?

The reality is this: most people don't have a clue about how powerful they really are. They'll never find out until they choose to move beyond being interested and make a commitment to give what they consider the impossible a shot.

Some people report feeling overwhelmed when they try to reach new goals. Others describe the sensation as being stuck. Still others say that they reached for a goal once and were unsuccessful, so they've given themselves enthusiastic permission not to try again.

Don't allow fear of failure to cause you to fail.

As with the players on the successful CBS television series *Survivor,* a commitment (to be the last person standing) often means doing what some people can't bring themselves to do, such as existing on bugs or slathering themselves in mud.

It's the same, whether you are setting a personal or a professional goal. Often you have to make the choice to commit passionately to do what others can't, or won't, do. The next step is investment of time, money, yourself, or whatever else is needed. Then be prepared to sacrifice.

What Is Passionate Commitment?

In 1921, history was made at Kane Summit Hospital in Pennsylvania. Veteran surgeon Dr. Evan O'Neill Kane performed an appendectomy using local anesthesia for the first time. Dr. Kane had been a crusader contending that local anesthesia was far safer than the conventional method of using general anesthesia. Not many of his colleagues believed his theory and were reluctant to test it on their patients. They needed proof.

Dr. Kane's patients were not excited about being a part of a laboratory study, either. After several weeks of searching for a volunteer to prove his theory, the surgeon finally found a candidate who was willing to test the theory while undergoing an appendectomy.

When it was time for the surgery, the patient was prepped and wheeled into the surgical suite. Dr. Kane then took the scalpel and performed the surgery. The procedure went as planned and the patient complained only of minor discomfort. Two days after the procedure, the patient was dismissed from the hospital ward. Thanks to the brave volunteer, Dr. Kane demonstrated that local anesthesia was not only a viable alternative to general anesthesia but also, even preferable.

Who was the courageous volunteer for Dr. Kane's experimental surgery? Dr. Kane, himself—he performed the first surgery using local anesthesia on himself. He was so committed to his belief that he was willing to become a patient in order to convince other patients to trust their doctor. Everyone else was interested in knowing if the procedure would work . . . Dr. Kane was committed to find out for himself.

Are you passionate enough about your personal and professional commitments to put yourself on the "gurney"?

Jumping In

January 2, 2007, was like most every other day in New York City. People were lined up along the subway platform waiting for the next train.

Cameron Hollopeter, a nineteen-year-old student, had a medical episode and fell onto the tracks into the path of a train headed into the station.

Wesley Autrey, a construction worker, was standing close by with his two daughters. He reached down and tried to rescue the teenager but could not get him back on the platform. Then Wesley faced a harrowing choice. Should he let Cameron go or jump in and risk his own life trying to save Cameron's?

Wesley was passionate enough about attempting to save Cameron's life that he made the ultimate commitment. Jumping down from the platform, he pinned down Cameron, keeping his limbs off the tracks while the train passed over them, with all of about two inches to spare.

"I did it out of a split-second reaction. And if I had to do it again, I probably would. It was like, 'Wow, I got to go get this guy . . . somebody's gotta save this guy,' but I was the closest one," said this modern-day hero.

A lot of interested people were standing on the platform,

but Cameron's life was saved because of Wesley's split-second reaction and his commitment to save a life.

Julie Moss

In 1982, the Ironman Triathlon was broadcast for the first time on NBC-TV. The bright sunshine of Hawaii's Kona Coast glittered on the backs of hundreds of athletes as they plunged into the ocean for the 2.5-mile swim. Once out of the water, they were on their way for a 100-mile bike ride around the island before completing the third leg, a 26.2-mile (marathon) run to the finish line. Any wonder why they call it Ironman?

Viewers who saw that race will never forget the images of twenty-three-year-old Julie Moss, crawling across the finish line in the darkness, totally dehydrated, her legs unable to support her for the final yards. This was her first Ironman competition, and her goal was to finish. She had dreamed of crossing the finish line, had envisioned herself waving to the crowd as she broke the tape.

Few would have suffered the humiliation of a body so out of control it could barely crawl, but Moss was committed to finishing—and she did, dragging herself and crawling over the finish line only twenty-nine seconds behind the first-place woman, Kathleen McCartney. Millions witnessed her feat and were inspired by her example.

Julie Moss was not just committed—she exhibited passionate commitment. So what do people who choose passionate commitment do?

In most cases, they aren't as battle-fatigued as Julie Moss, but they often make great sacrifices to reach their goals. Here are a few of the attributes of people who have passionate commitment:

- They do what they say they'll do because they have made the commitment to do it. You can count on them every time. When they tell you they will do something, you can consider it done.

- Like Julie Moss, they believe so strongly they can achieve a goal that they can envision themselves crossing the finish line. They can vividly see success.

- They write and verbalize their commitments. This doesn't mean sitting around talking about what they plan to do. They put their goals into words and then get busy.

- They're realistic. They don't over-promise and under-deliver. Whatever they say, you can believe it.

- People who choose commitment invest in achieving their goals. They may invest the classroom time necessary to earn a college degree, energy on the basketball court practicing three-pointers, or hours at the computer pounding out that first novel. When they commit, they invest.

- Committed people don't beat themselves up for falling short. They use that experience to learn and continue the process.

- People who choose to commit always plan their lives around what it takes to achieve a goal. They are focused, and they make their success a top priority.

- Most committed people don't understand the term "fail." They think it means "one step closer to success."

- Like Julie Moss, people who commit themselves to a goal have an impact on the lives of those around them. Enthusiasm and commitment are contagious.

Do you possess any of these attributes? Of course you do. We all have dreams and goals. We all want to move ahead, higher, or farther down life's road.

The difference between those who achieve their goals and those who set them aside is the choice of commitment: being passionate enough to succeed.

Three Things You Can Do to Make the Commitment Choice

1. Stay the course. If your goal is worth committing to, it is worth the price that comes with passionate commitment.

2. Surround yourself with people who are equally committed—and passionate.

3. Clarify your commitment. Put your goals into words, and then begin making your commitment a reality. Always be able to answer in fewer than twenty words what you want to accomplish in the next two years.

Monday Morning Discussion Questions

1. Do you have to be passionate about something to be committed?

2. Can you be committed to both work and family at the same time?

3. Name a person who is an inspiration to you. Describe the traits of that person. Are "passionate" and "committed" two of the traits you described?

Words of Wisdom about the Commitment Choice

When work, commitment, and pleasure all become one, and you reach that deep well where passion lives, nothing is impossible.

ANONYMOUS

If you don't love what you do, you have two choices. You can either change what you're doing or you can change what you love.

BILLY COX

Standing in the middle of the road is very dangerous; you get knocked down by traffic from both sides.

MARGARET THATCHER

To be successful, you have to have your heart in your business and your business in your heart.

THOMAS WATSON, SR.

The happiness of a man in this life does not consist in the absence, but in the mastery, of his passions.

ALFRED LORD TENNYSON

There is one quality that one must possess to win, and that is definiteness of purpose—the knowledge of what one wants and a burning desire to possess it.

NAPOLEON HILL

If you can dream it, you can do it. Never lose sight of the fact that this whole thing was started by a mouse.

WALT DISNEY

The Values Choice . . .
Choose the Right Enemies

A wise man learns more from his enemies than a fool from his friends.
BALTASAR GRACIAN

Jackson Klein's hard work was paying off. He had just been promoted to VP of sales and was settling into his corner office.

Right after his appointment to VP had been announced, Rudy Russell, a mentor and confidant, had joined Jackson for lunch and reminded him of something Rudy had experienced in his own career: "When you move into that corner office, you'll be everybody's friend and hero," Rudy had counseled. "However, I advise you to be prepared to lose friends—and make enemies—with every decision you make after you've unloaded the last box."

The new VP had thought about Rudy's advice and decided his vice presidency was going to be different. After all, he hadn't gotten this high in the organization without learning how to please most of his customers most of the time.

About a month later, it dawned on Jackson just how right his mentor had been. Whether his decisions involved something as trivial as the color of new business cards for the sales group or as significant as hiring members to expand the sales team, there were always critics who disagreed with his every move.

Rudy was right. Jackson had moved into his new position surrounded by well-wishers and what some would characterize as raving fans. In less than six weeks, the line had been drawn in the sand—those who supported Jackson and those who couldn't wait to see him leave.

Later, over another lunch, Rudy gave Jackson just the advice he needed to move forward in his career and in his life. "My grandfather used to tell us, 'Hold your friends close and your enemies closer,' said Jackson's mentor. "I always thought that was strange advice, but I've followed it several times in my own career. What I learned was this: by getting to know your enemies, you soon figure out how they think, how they react, and that can help you stay a step ahead when it comes time for the race."

Jackson nodded. "That makes sense."

"The other advice I learned from my grandmother," Rudy continued. "She was a proud woman, who always wanted the best for my father and his brothers. One day she found out my dad was running with a rough crowd, so that evening she took him aside and told him, 'Either walk with the tallest or walk alone.' My grandmother was a plain-spoken woman, and my dad immediately got her message. Never compromise your values, even if it means going it alone, because it will pay off later."

Jackson took those two gems of wisdom and incorporated them into his own relationships. When he left the VP's office to take his next promotion, he left with more friends than enemies but with the respect of all those who knew him well. Not once in his tenure had he ever compromised his values.

Values are defined as the accepted principles or standards of an individual or group. Knowing what they are is different from actually living by them. It's a continuous test.

Even though you understand what your values are, there will be conflict when you have to make choices. So stand by your values.

Unfortunately, that will sometimes lead to enemies.

By the time most people have lived long enough to become adults, they've accumulated more than a few enemies—probably even more than they'd like to admit.

Enemies normally surface because of a values clash. The values you have chosen to be a nonnegotiable part of your life are in conflict with someone else's values.

It is interesting to note that our civilization has used the word "enemy" at least since the thirteenth century, with meanings that include the following:

1. one who is antagonistic to another; especially one seeking to injure, overthrow, or confound an opponent
2. something harmful or deadly
3. a military adversary or a hostile unit or force

No matter which definition you use, the more successful you become, the more enemies you're going to have.

There Will Be Enemies for Many Reasons

One Sunday morning while preaching on the theme "Love Thy Enemies," the late Dr. Martin Luther King, Jr. told his congregation flatly, "The fact is, some people will not like you, not because of something you have done to them, but they just won't like you. Some people aren't going to like the way you walk; some people aren't going to like the way you talk. Some people aren't going to like you because you can do your job better than they can do theirs.

"Some people aren't going to like you because other people like you, and because you're popular, and because you're well-liked, they aren't going to like you," Dr. King continued. "Some people aren't going to like you because your hair is a little shorter than theirs or your hair is a little longer, and some are going to dislike you, not because of something that you've done to them, but because of various jealous reactions and other reactions that are so prevalent in human nature."

The question is not whether there will be enemies. You can't please everybody. You cannot invest your self-worth solely in what others think about you. You would never achieve success. Keep focused on your goals and objectives, and when the enemies come along, don't be surprised, but welcome them. Enemies are a by-product of success. The more successful you are in your career, the more susceptible you are to critics and a growing number of enemies, both inside and outside your office building.

As the old saying has it, "You can please all of the people some of the time and some of the people all the time, but you cannot please all the people all the time."

Even as we work to succeed, it is human nature to want to be accepted and respected—even loved—by our co-workers, management, and customers. However, the truth is that we can't please everyone all of the time. At some point you have to choose whom you're not going to please.

Choosing Your Values

I have had to make the values choice in my career on more than one occasion, and I have found that it's not always an easy choice.

I was fortunate to be on a fast track almost my entire career while working for Xerox and FedEx. I enjoyed every job and was relatively successful in every assignment. Yet, while I was moving up the corporate ladder I had to make some personal value choices.

In one step up that ladder, my choice was to uproot my

family and move six hundred miles north. I had three children in school at the time, but I thought it would be no big deal to make the move. My three children were in the ninth, seventh, and second grades.

I had a "family board meeting" and discussed the new opportunity. Excited, I explained about the fresh start, more money, new house, new friends, and everything else I thought was significant.

I was shocked! Only one person (me) was in favor of the move. No one else in my family thought any of those things was important.

Important to the kids were school, friends, and being close to extended family. Important to Karen, my wife, was being close to her mother, who was in ill health at that time.

That's when I had to choose between important, yet very different values. I could justify the move and enjoy the promotion and money—after all, it was for the "betterment of my family." They would adjust and stick with me, whatever my decision. But the question I had to ask myself was "What's really important?"

If enemies were made by this decision, who would I rather the enemies be? My family or my boss?

So, I made the choice to turn down the job. It was one of the best choices of my career. I gained respect from friends and co-workers when I stood up for my personal values, even when there was a price to be paid. My boss, whom I was worried would become an enemy, resigned within a year and was no longer around.

I had chosen my potential enemies, and I definitely didn't want them living under the same roof.

No Need to Create Enemies . . . They Will Surface on Their Own

In no way am I suggesting that your goal should be to create enemies. I do encourage you to understand that others may choose to be your enemies. They may be jealous of your success, or they may not like the fact that you do your job better than they do theirs. It may be that their values don't match yours.

In many organizations, a handful of individuals seemingly thrive on controversy and seek out ways to create and inflame disputes. These are the enemies you will be forced to choose, people who are in conflict with your personal values.

People who disagree with you are not necessarily your enemies unless their disagreement centers on the values you are trying to uphold. Whatever the consequences, never sacrifice your values—but be aware that you'll create enemies by making such a choice.

So, ask the question, Who are my enemies? It's a question that deserves thought.

In any business, the key to successfully dealing with your enemies is being able to identify who they are and to understand why they have chosen to be your enemies.

If they are enemies because they are jealous or threatened by your success, there is nothing you can do about it. If they are your enemies because of something you've done to them in the past, address the situation and allow them the choice of leaving your enemy camp.

If you have done everything you can to allow the enemies to choose to be allies and they still choose to be enemies, move forward. Chasing after a poisonous snake that has bitten you will not solve the problem. It is far better to move in a direction away from the snake and allow the snake to go its own way.

Be aware—mistaking an enemy for an ally is the most foolish and costly mistake of all.

It Matters Whom We Hang With

As any parent would attest, one of the most important decisions made by their children is their choice of friends. Bad choices made by teenagers can have a potentially devastating impact on their lives.

Our choice of who we hang with at work is just as important as our teenagers' choice of friends.

How important is it to identify and choose our enemies, avoiding the corrupting influence of those who do not respect or hold our values?

Here's a story to illustrate the answer. Centuries ago, the slave Aesop penned a fable about a mouse who always lived on the land. By an unlucky chance, this mouse formed an intimate acquaintance with a frog who, for the most part, lived in the water.

One day, the frog was intent on mischief. He tied the foot of the mouse tightly to his own. While they were thus joined together, the frog led his friend the mouse to the meadow where they usually searched for food. Gradually, the frog led the mouse toward the pond in which he lived. Then, upon reaching the banks of the water, the frog suddenly jumped in, dragging the mouse with him.

Enjoying the water immensely, the frog swam, croaking about, as if he had done a good deed. The unhappy mouse soon sputtered and drowned. His poor dead body floated on the surface.

A hawk observed the floating mouse from the sky and dived down and grabbed it with his talons, carrying it back to his nest. The frog, still fastened to the leg of the mouse, was also carried off a prisoner and was eaten by the hawk.

The moral: It is important to choose wisely who you associate with. The wrong person will lead you down the wrong path or into the wrong pond. Unfortunately, those of us not equipped to swim will inevitably drown.

Values—a Defining Difference

What makes us different from the enemies we choose?

The defining difference is our values, but you must learn, and learn quickly, who shares your values and who places little worth on doing the right thing.

Other "enemies" in business—and in life—worth choosing are these:

- Backstabbers—those who betray a confidence or those who constantly discredit others

- People with short tempers—they are often catalysts for anger and discord at any moment

- Those who lose control by drinking too much at business functions

- Rebels against authority—they are on a collision course with failure

- People who rarely do what they say they are going to do

Choose your enemies and your friends very carefully. A bad choice can be devastating to your career.

Three Things You Can Do to Make the Values Choice

1. Surround yourself with people of like values, and maintain your allegiance to those values.
2. Take the time to identify those who have chosen to be your enemies, and make an effort to understand why. If they are your enemies because of something you have done in the past, address the situation. If they are your enemies because of jealousy or a values clash, move forward with caution, knowing they are your enemies.
3. Understand that you cannot please all the people

all the time, and accept that differences in values will automatically make some people your friends and others your enemies.

Monday Morning Discussion Questions

1. Why does success create enemies?

2. Describe what values you have that are nonnegotiable, at work and at home.

3. Is it possible for enemies to make us stronger and better?

Words of Wisdom about
the Values Choice

There is a time when we must firmly choose the course we will follow, or the relentless drift of events will make the decision for us.

HERBERT B. PROCHNOW

Associate yourself with men of good quality if you esteem your own reputation, for 'tis better to be alone than in bad company.

GEORGE WASHINGTON

To be wronged is nothing unless you continue to remember it.

CONFUCIUS

Always forgive your enemies—nothing annoys them so much.

OSCAR WILDE

If we could read the secret history of our enemies, we should find in each man's life sorrow and suffering enough to disarm all hostility.

HENRY WADSWORTH LONGFELLOW

Keep away from people who try to belittle your ambition. Small people always do that, but the really great make you feel that you, too, can become great.

MARK TWAIN

I have found that the greatest help in meeting any problem with decency and self-respect and whatever courage is demanded, is to know where you yourself stand. That is, to have in words what you believe and are acting from.

WILLIAM FAULKNER

Wounds from a friend can be trusted, but an enemy multiplies kisses.

PROVERBS 27:6 (NIV)

Keeping score of old scores and scars, getting even and one-upping, always make you less than you are.

MALCOLM FORBES

Monday Morning Choice #4

The Integrity Choice . . .
Do the Right Thing

A good name is more desirable than great riches;
to be esteemed is better than silver or gold.
PROVERBS 22:1 (NIV)

The late J. C. Penney, founder of the JCPenney stores, was known for his integrity. In his book *View from the Ninth Decade* he tells of working at the village grocery as a boy and reporting to his father about how the grocer would mix two grades of coffee and sell the mixture at the higher price. Young Penney thought this was a smart trick, but his father pointed out that the practice was dishonest, making his point so strongly that the boy quit his job. From that time on, Penney made honesty and integrity the foundation of his decisions throughout his lifetime.

Integrity is defined in the dictionary as "the quality of possessing and steadfastly adhering to high moral principles or professional standards." My definition is "never being ashamed of my reflection."

How important is integrity? No quality reveals a person's true character more than integrity. It is the cornerstone of our personal and professional lives.

Whom Do You Trust?

Stop right now and make a list of five individuals you consider trustworthy. They may be family members, friends, business associates, teachers, clergy, or community leaders—they can be anyone, as long as you trust them. Write their names:

1.
2.
3.
4.
5.

Now look at your list and ask yourself, "What characteristics do these people have in common?"

They likely share honesty and integrity.

Now, think of five people you don't trust. What traits do these individuals share? You probably think of them as dishonest, or perhaps you question their integrity.

One thing most everyone will agree on is that if you sacrifice your integrity, nothing else really matters. After all, does it matter what you say to people if they don't trust you? Does it matter how committed, optimistic, skilled at resolving conflicts, or courageous you are if people do not trust you?

None of these traits really matters if your integrity is questionable. It simply makes no difference how great your intentions are. If there is little or no trust, there is no foundation for a successful relationship.

People with integrity possess one of the most respected virtues in the world. If you are a person of integrity who can be trusted, you set yourself apart. If you are truly a person of your word and convictions, you are unique and valued by others.

Honesty, integrity, and trust are inextricably linked. If people perceive you to be a person of integrity, you will earn their trust over time. Someone once said, "People of integrity expect to be believed, and when they're not, they let time prove them right."

Many times, the loss of integrity becomes the difference between failure and success, between sorrow and happiness. The integrity choice—doing the right thing regardless of who is watching—is one of the most important choices you will ever make, personally or professionally.

Since the collapse of several mega corporations and public figures in the United States, the word "integrity" has become a nonnegotiable descriptor for leaders and employees in any discipline, from medicine and research to banking, real estate, manufacturing, sales, and any other endeavor.

Think back over your past experiences. If you are like most people, some of your greatest disappointments have come when you heard people you trusted saying they were going to do something or telling you they had done something, only to find later that they hadn't. Or they could be people who like to "put one over" on the team, the boss, or even you, believing they can do anything they wish as long as they don't get caught.

Getting caught has nothing to do with integrity. Integrity is doing the right thing, even if there is no chance you would be caught doing the wrong thing.

Integrity is our foundation. Everything we do reflects our integrity, whether we are making personal decisions or decisions involving our organization.

How Important Is Integrity?

When you install a new software program on your computer, it will automatically run what is called an integrity check—a series of tests to determine whether any part of the program has been lost or damaged. If any piece of the code in that program doesn't have complete integrity, the program as a whole can't be trusted. At best, you would have a program that wasn't functioning properly. At worst, using a program lacking integrity could cause you to lose valuable data or even damage your computer, so the integrity check is vital.

But as the pace of business gains even more speed, thanks in part to the integrity of our computer programs, we are paying less attention to personal integrity. For instance, when it is discovered that a politician lacks integrity, we are no longer surprised. In fact, we actually expect it.

Closer to home, many people are encouraged to do whatever it takes to claw their way to the top and to ignore personal principles in favor of status symbols like the big house in the gated community, the BMW, and the Rolex. Some business leaders don't think twice about lying to get their point across, and these so-called white lies, along with shortcuts and "stretching the truth," are commonplace in our boardrooms.

What has happened? This lack of integrity has created skepticism, and people have become more cynical. The truth is that when it comes to integrity, there is no gray area. *Integrity is the principal trait for long-term success.*

A Large Dose of Integrity

In the fall of 1982, seven people on the west side of Chicago mysteriously died. Investigators found that each of the victims had ingested an extra-strength Tylenol capsule before dying—capsules that were found to be laced with cyanide.

News of these incidents traveled fast, causing a massive nationwide panic. A typical corporation's response might have been to minimize the issue and start looking for others to blame for the problem.

Officials at McNeil Consumer Products, a subsidiary of Johnson & Johnson—makers of Tylenol—made a tough choice, one that tested their integrity.

They acted quickly, immediately alerting consumers

across the nation not to consume any type of Tylenol product. Then, along with halting production and any Tylenol advertising, Johnson & Johnson's top management recalled approximately 31 million bottles of Tylenol with a retail value of more than $100 million.

All of the major newscasts focused on shelf after shelf of Tylenol products being swept into large plastic bags for disposal. It was a time of humiliation for Johnson & Johnson.

A few days later, Johnson & Johnson offered to exchange all Tylenol capsules that already had been purchased for new Tylenol tablets at a cost of several million dollars more to the corporation. Immediately thereafter, the company offered a $100,000 reward for the capture of the individual or individuals involved in the tampering case.

In addition, when the Johnson & Johnson team developed a tamper-proof cap, it gave its competitors the specifications of the cap so they could use it, too.

Without a doubt, Johnson & Johnson had put customer safety first before worrying about the company's profit and other financial concerns. They passed the integrity test. Their actions became the benchmark of corporate integrity—doing the right thing, regardless of the consequences.

Through the company's actions, it became obvious that Johnson & Johnson only wanted to do the right thing, once the link between Tylenol and the seven deaths in Chicago had been established. Through their actions, Johnson & Johnson's top management let the nation know that, whatever the costs, they would choose integrity. This choice ul-

timately served them well as they sought to reestablish the
nation's confidence in their products.

Why the Integrity Choice Is Important

As with every other choice we've discussed, a person who
chooses integrity will enrich lives, relationships, and success
in every endeavor.

Dishonesty—the opposite of integrity—often carries a
lasting and unpleasant aftertaste. In many arenas, dishonesty
is the basis for both individual and corporate downfall. Rarely
does the individual who operates without integrity find long-
term success.

Integrity is also not something that can be practiced only
part of the time, only when we're thinking about it, or only
with certain people.

Peter Scotese, chairman emeritus of New York's Fashion
Institute of Technology, stated it best when he said, "Integrity is not a 90 percent thing, not a 95 percent thing—either
you have it or you don't."

Scotese learned about integrity early in life. His father
died the same year Peter was born, in 1920. When he was
eight, his mother enrolled him in a school for orphaned boys,
where he washed dishes, cleaned buildings, and waited tables
in return for his education.

After serving in World War II, earning the Bronze Star
and two Purple Hearts, he began a career in textiles at Indian
Head Mills of New York before moving to Springs Industries, Inc., in 1969, becoming the first nonfamily president

of that corporation. During his tenure, sales tripled and earnings quadrupled.

In 1981, Scotese was the recipient of the Horatio Alger Foundation Award. He was recognized as an outstanding American, demonstrating individual initiative and a commitment to excellence, exemplified by remarkable achievements accomplished through honesty, hard work, self-reliance, and perseverance. In his acceptance speech, he attributed his success to the way integrity had empowered his life.

Doing the right thing and being honest in all of his business dealings were the principal factors that led to his success.

Why Success Relies on Integrity

In any successful team effort, we find ourselves relying on the integrity of our teammates. We have to commit to certain efforts and then carry through on that commitment. We have to share a level of integrity that forbids cutting corners, letting things slip through the cracks, or performing less than 100 percent of what we say we will do. A successful team is the result of connected independence based on the integrity of each team member.

The same holds true for customers. When customers place orders they rely on the integrity of their sales representatives and the integrity of companies to receive the quality they expect.

In many cases, it is easier to over-promise and under-deliver. Popular mottoes of business are "Success at all costs" and "Whatever it takes." However, business leaders are often quick to learn that practices lacking integrity soon lose business and sometimes cost them their business.

Never abide by "Success at all costs," particularly if the cost of doing business is a compromise of personal or corporate integrity.

Word of Caution

Everyone wrestles with the integrity choice at one time or another. External pressures create questions about how important our integrity really is . . . or who will know, anyway?

Here is the caution: Integrity is usually lost in small choices, the ones that seem insignificant at the time. Most people do not make a conscious decision to sacrifice their integrity by making one big, bad mistake. It is the accumulation of bad choices, all of which seem minor, that leads to the next bad choice.

It's like the story of how to boil a frog. If you throw a frog into a pot of boiling water, he will leap out immediately because he realizes the danger and knows that he does not want to be in the boiling water. Yet, if you put the same frog in a pot of cold water and slowly turn up the heat, the frog will never realize the subtle changes in temperature and will remain in the pot until it reaches 212 degrees—boiling. If allowed, he will stay in the pot until he is boiled to well done.

That's how integrity is lost: one degree of dishonesty at a time. Many times the loser is not even aware of the severity of the situation.

Succeed with Integrity

What are the characteristics of people with integrity, who can be trusted when they give their word about anything?

- They establish integrity as a top priority. It is the cornerstone of their actions and decisions.

- They have clear, uncompromised values and communicate them without hesitation.

- They do what is right and ethical regardless of the circumstances—no hidden agendas, no games, and no regrets.

- They never compromise their integrity by rationalizing a situation as "an isolated incident." There are no "isolated incidents." These people decide where their integrity boundaries exist, and they stay within them.

- They never allow achieving results to become more important than the means to their achievement. How they win is just as important as winning.

- They do what they say they will do. Their integrity is judged every time they say they make a commitment, regardless of its significance.

The choice of integrity is one of the most important choices you can make, because integrity not only guides every action but also chooses the paths necessary for long-term success. There is never a good reason to sacrifice your integrity! People will forgive and forget judgment errors, but they never forget integrity mistakes.

Trust is a by-product of integrity. Somewhere along the way, as you seek wealth, knowledge, success, or votes, your integrity will be put to the test. Choose to do the right thing, even if it hurts.

Three Things You Can Do to Make the Integrity Choice

1. Guard your integrity as though it were your most important possession . . . because that is exactly what it is!

2. Realize that there are no time-outs with your integrity. It is also not something that can be practiced only part of the time, or only with certain people. Protecting your integrity is an all-the-time deal.

3. Do the right thing. It isn't always easy—in fact, sometimes it's the most difficult of all options. But just remember, doing the right thing is always right.

Monday Morning Discussion Questions

1. When is our integrity challenged at work?

2. Is it possible to be absolutely honest with every person?

3. Can you give an example of when a person lost everything because of losing integrity?

Words of Wisdom about the Integrity Choice

There is no pillow as soft as a clear conscience.

JOHN WOODEN

One of the most striking differences between a cat and a lie is that a cat has only nine lives.

MARK TWAIN

Integrity is the commitment to do what is right regardless of the circumstances—no hidden agendas, no political games. Do the right thing, period.

KEN CARNES

Truth has no special time of its own. Its hour is now— always.

ALBERT SCHWEITZER

It is no use walking anywhere to preach unless our walking is our preaching.

ST. FRANCIS OF ASSISI

In matters of style, swim with the current; in matters of principle, stand like a rock.

THOMAS JEFFERSON

To see what is right and not to do it is cowardice.

CONFUCIUS

Anyone who thinks they can go to the top and stay there without being honest is dumb.

MORTIMA FEINBERG

Until you make peace with who you are, you'll never be content with what you have.

DORIS MORTMAN

There can be no happiness if the things we believe in are different from the things we do.

FREYA STARK

What lies behind us and what lies before us are tiny matters compared to what lies within us.

RALPH WALDO EMERSON

Part II

Action Choices: The Movement Toward Success

A man is the sum of his actions, of what he has done, of what he can do. Nothing else.

MAHATMA GANDHI

The Do-Something Choice. . . Don't Vacation on "Someday Isle"

Have you ever said: "Someday I'll be happy when . . .
I lose twenty pounds, live in a bigger house . . .
get a new boyfriend/girlfriend . . . make more money, etc. ?"
Someday Isle is not a dream vacation spot. It is an imaginary destination
to which you will never arrive. It is the carrot on the stick perpetually
in front of you. So close you can see it, yet you will never reach it.
Don't vacation on Someday Isle.
FRANK F. LUNN, AUTHOR OF *STACK THE LOGS!*

Quick! Answer this riddle: Three frogs are sitting on a lily pad. One decides to jump off. How many frogs remain on the lily pad?

If you said three, you're right. Deciding to jump off and actually doing it are two completely different things.

The most powerful engine in the world will not generate any movement until someone has the knowledge, ability, and desire to start it up. Once started, the engine can take you into space. Your career is the same. You can have all the talent in the world, but you will not generate any upward movement until you decide to put the talent into action.

Intentions Do Not Count

A day seldom passes without someone telling me that he or she wants to write a book. The person has a good idea and the desire to make a difference in others' lives. My advice is always the same: Great! People would love to hear your story, so do it!

Writing a book takes time, commitment, and passion. It is done mainly in solitude. As twentieth-century American writer William Faulkner found, it also takes persuasive persistence to get the words on paper.

Most of the time, that great book remains an intention and never gets written. Seldom is a chapter written, and most of the time not a word is written on paper. That person may have a great book inside his or her head and may have decided to write a book, but the book will not write itself. Such people are vacationing on Someday Isle.

How do you leave this vacation spot? Get going and do something!

How many times this week did you decide to do something and then not follow through? For many people, this is a routine choice—but how often have they looked back, regretting that they didn't pursue a goal, or take the time to explore a new idea, because they were waiting for some better day or time.

To achieve success, you have to make the choice to do something different. The disparity between those who choose to take initiative and do something that will lead to success as opposed to those who only talk about what they would like to happen is the difference between night and day. I am not talking about a 10 percent, a 20 percent, or even a 50 percent difference. The difference is beyond measure!

Never be content with the status quo. The status quo may be comfortable, but you cannot improve while you are in the rut of doing the same things over and over. My friend Brian Tracy once told me that "the only difference between a rut and a grave is the depth . . . and the first thing you do when you get into a rut is to quit digging."

Intending to get out of the rut does not count! You have to do something to get out and move forward.

The Donkey and the Well

One day a donkey fell into a well. When the owner discovered what had happened, he frantically searched for ways to rescue the animal but with no success. Regrettably, the owner finally decided that since the donkey was growing old, he should give up the idea of rescuing the animal and simply fill in the well. Hopefully, the donkey's demise would be quick and painless.

The farmer then called his neighbors to help with the task, and soon several men began shoveling dirt into the well.

When the donkey realized what was happening, he brayed and struggled . . . but finally the noise stopped.

After a few sad moments, the farmer looked into the well, and there stood the donkey. Alive and progressing to the top, the donkey had found that by shaking off the dirt instead of allowing it to bury him, he could keep stepping on top of the earth as its level rose. Then he easily stepped out of the well and happily trotted off.

As you may have noticed, life often attempts to cover us over with dirt and clutter . . . mostly clutter. The trick is to shake it off and do something to take the next step up.

Do Something to Change Your Life— Read Every Day

One of the principal reasons for creating *Monday Morning Choices* was to challenge you to get into the habit of reading. It can change your life. Twenty years ago, it changed my life when I began reading at least a book a month, and I discovered, firsthand, that the more I learned the more I earned. You can make the same discovery.

Do you think it's coincidental that, in most cases, the bigger the house, the bigger the library inside the house? It is not coincidental! There is a direct correlation between the books you read and the success you achieve. The more you learn, the more opportunities you will have to earn.

Charlie "Tremendous" Jones, my friend and wise counsel, says, "You are today what you'll be five years from now, except for the people you meet and the books you read."

Think about that. In five years, you can be completely different or just like you are right now. It's your choice. Career success requires you to continue increasing your knowledge. Many top executives read up to ten books a month; yet, the average American, after completing the last year of formal education, will probably not read ten books in a lifetime.

Peter Drucker said, "Knowledge has to be improved, challenged, and increased constantly or it vanishes." Successful people understand that principle and enjoy becoming lifelong learners. The habit of reading becomes contagious to those surrounding them.

The next time you visit someone's home, check out the books on the table next to his or her favorite chair. See what kinds of books are on the bookshelves. You can tell what has molded the philosophy and values of a person by the books he or she reads.

The good news? An abundance of books is available to teach or inform you about any subject you can name.

Would you like to sit down and talk to Albert Einstein? Then read one of his essays. What would you like to ask Winston Churchill about his life experiences? Pick up any of hundreds of books and read how he would answer your question. Would you enjoy hearing Ronald Reagan tell how it felt to tell Mikhail Gorbachev "Tear down this wall!"? Read his memoirs. How about listening to Peter Drucker talk about management and leadership? Read his books. Or if you want to become a more complete thinker, read the Bible, as the vast majority of great thinkers have done, whether or not they believed its messages.

You may be limited in the people you will meet in your lifetime. Many of the people you would like to meet and enjoy learning from are not available. But you are not limited in what you can learn from others. Reward yourself with the knowledge of great people, and become a better person because of the information that awaits you in books.

Where do you start? Anywhere. Just start enjoying the company of the greats or the pleasure of exploring your interests by reading!

I suggest that people read Fred Smith's *You and Your Network*. That book was written over fifty years ago, but the wisdom it contains is timeless and can be the launching pad for helping you get the most out of your life and your career. Start with that book, or start somewhere else. It does not matter where you start. Once you begin the habit of reading and discover the rewards of knowledge, you will make it a permanent part of your life.

Go to the library or online. You can even visit my Web site, www.CornerStoneLeadership.com, where we offer hundreds of books. The point is this: you have to make the choice and create a habit of reading. No one can do it for you. Just get started!

During my career I have hired hundreds of recent college graduates. After studying and evaluating the difference between the successful ones and those who did not make it in business, I discovered one simple common denominator among those who fail: they think their learning is complete when they get their diplomas. They quit investing in learning. The graduates who achieve long-term success are those who have the discipline to continue to spend hours every day, even in their later career years, learning and improving.

The more you learn, the more you will be able to earn. It is your choice. Don't go through a day without reading. It will change your life.

The Best Keep Doing Something to Become Even Better

People can be divided into three categories: those who make things happen, those who watch things happen, and those who wonder what happened.

Successful people make things happen by taking action and not allowing themselves to be swept along by what life brings.

There are plenty of great examples of how the "do-something" choice works. Take a look at some of the many athletes who made the choice to do something, even though they were already the best in the world.

Olympian Carl Lewis, even after setting world records in track and field, made the choice to continue working and training with his college coach so he could run a little faster and jump farther than his last record.

After dominating the junior tournaments, long after

other golfers had gone into the clubhouse, young Tiger Woods remained on the course, practicing his shots. He was not content just to win. He chose instead to do whatever it took to be the best to ever play the game of golf.

Most successful people are never satisfied with their last score, their last record, or their last performance. How many great authors have written just one book? How many great leaders have quit after one successful year? How many great coaches have quit after their first win?

Learn from the best. They keep learning and searching for ways to become even better.

Winners Keep Winning

Early in my career, while I was working for Xerox, one of my yearly goals was to win the annual President's Club award. Each year, the top corporate performers would be recognized with a great trip. After I had enjoyed a couple of those President's Club trips, one of my observations was that 80 percent (my estimate) of the winners were the same people every year.

Were all those repeat winners just the lucky salespeople with the best territories? Of course not. Many changed territories multiple times but still made the President's Club trip. Their "luck" was in making the choice to keep getting better, even though they were already at the top of their fields.

In the years since that observation, I have confirmed that the winners keep winning, whatever the business. A tough year may come along occasionally, but over the long haul, winners keep winning because they keep doing the necessary "somethings" to win.

Rarely is anything gained by spending too much time soaking up the limelight of that last success. You have to continue to make the "do-something" choice!

Do Something to Clearly Communicate

Regardless of the career you choose, to be successful you have to be able to get your point across.

Fair or not, people tend to judge you by how well you speak, write, and listen. Every word spoken, every sentence written, and every instance of how well you listen send a message. The message you want to send is this: I am committed to succeed! It's a proven fact: your chances for success will increase in proportion to the strength of your vocabulary and your ability to communicate.

More than any other single attribute, the use of a well-rounded vocabulary is an immediate indication of your intelligence. Ironically, most people's vocabularies stagnate before the age of thirty.

Being able to speak to groups of two or three or even to a roomful is required for advancement in almost every industry. Opinions are always formed on the basis of how well you deliver a message. The message may be as simple as "Say a few words about yourself" or as important as "Tell us why your team needs a budget increase."

Successful people spend time and energy to focus on improving their verbal communication skills.

A second communication skill required for success is the ability to write clearly and concisely. What and how you write represents you. Those who receive your memos, e-mails, reports, and other documents automatically form an impression of you.

The ability to listen effectively is a third communication skill required for success that is often overlooked. Studies have shown that miscommunication occurs largely because people do not take the time to listen.

What can you do to improve your communication skills?

Plenty of choices are available. Communication classes are given online or at your local college, public speaking groups are easily found, writing courses are abundant, and, of course, there are books on every communication subject. Choose whatever fits your schedule. Just do something to become an effective communicator.

Doing Something Takes Courage

The difference between those who succeed and those who allow fear to immobilize them is the choice to courageously keep moving forward when things get tough.

Throughout literature, the theme of "courage" is second only to the theme of "love." Most of us would readily admit that courage is the one virtue we want for ourselves.

"If I had one wish," wrote a Harvard scholar, "it would

be never to be scared and never to feel the shame of being scared."

Sure, everybody has fears. From the part-time employee at the local car wash to the moguls who shape and guide corporations, we all fear the unknown, and we all fear failure.

When you make the choice to do something, your fear will diminish, your confidence will increase, and in the process you will remove the unknown. Attack what you fear, and the fear will eventually disappear.

One of the greatest mistakes you can make is to be paralyzed by the fear of making a mistake. The key to overcoming fear is to continue moving forward despite your fears.

Historically, the survivors of any great challenge are those who have kept moving forward. From the survivors of the ill-fated wagon train who found their way through the blizzards of Donner Pass to modern-day hiker Aron Ralston, who chose to keep moving by amputating his arm with a pocketknife after being pinned under an eight-hundred-pound boulder for five days, doing nothing would have been fatal. "Dying wasn't an alternative," Ralston said, after freeing himself and walking five miles before being found by two hikers who helped him to safety.

Doing nothing can be fatal to your success. Make the same choice as Aron Ralston and keep moving forward, in spite of your fears.

Move Forward

But some give up too soon, just before they turn the corner to success. Successful people keep moving, even when they are scared and have made mistakes. Unsuccessful people quit before they have a chance to be successful.

Every successful life story has at least two aspects that contributed to the person's success. One aspect is having the energy to do the things necessary to achieve success. The other aspect is having enough stability to stand through the challenges that reaching upward to "do-something" creates. Most people have the energy to do something to improve their situation; yet, many do not have the stability to continue to move forward toward success and plow through the challenges along the way.

Don't allow yourself to be stopped just short of success. Keep moving forward. In almost every situation, something can be done to improve the situation. There is something that you can do!

Do Something to Look Successful

One "do-something" choice everyone can make is to look successful. If you want to *be* successful, one of the first things you have to do is *look* successful.

The two things that immediately influence other people are the expression on your face and the clothes you wear. Even if you don't think you have the money to spend on expensive clothes, buy the best you can afford. Think of the clothes you wear and how you dress as an investment in your success.

In competitive situations, the candidate who looks healthy, happy, and energetic always has a better chance of being promoted. You don't have to be an Adonis to win a promotion, but it is definitely to your advantage to take care of each aspect of your life—physical, emotional, spiritual, and intellectual—and apply a dab of shoe polish. Making sure that shirt you plan to wear tomorrow is clean and pressed helps, too. Take a look around. The people you admire and respect are usually those who look and act like people worthy of admiration and respect.

Do something to look successful. If you feel unattractive, have a makeover. If you want to wear a smaller size, exercise and lose the weight. If you want to feel more energized, take a brisk walk every morning before work. It's amazing how those endorphins you create with exercise will make you feel. Choose to do something for yourself.

I'll Try versus Consider It Done

In the movie *The Empire Strikes Back,* Yoda says to Luke Sky-walker, "You must unlearn what you have learned."

Luke says, "Okay, I'll try."

"Try not," Yoda exclaimed, "Do . . . or do not. There is no 'try.'"

There is a big difference between "I'll try" and "I'll do." "I'll try" is often used as an excuse for not doing.

My assistant for seven years, Sheri Durham, was always

positive and upbeat. Three of the most comforting words that she consistently said to me when given a task were "Consider it done." I knew when I heard those words that there was no "try." I could chalk up the task as already done.

Eliminate the words "I'll try" from your vocabulary. There is no commitment to actually doing something when you use those words. The message you are sending with "I'll try" is weak. Tell others what you intend to do, and commit to getting it done.

Pay Attention

Finally, choose to do something that will make a difference. If you aren't happy with the way things are now, choose to do something about it.

Want a better tomorrow? Do something different today. Whatever is on your mind today will ultimately be in your future. Changing your life could be as simple as changing your mind when you make the choice to do something. If you have time to whine and complain about anything, you have time to do something about it.

One of the most important decisions you can make is to study what successful people do. Pay attention. What are the common "do-something" choices of the people who represent success to you? The choices they make are probably the same choices you can make to get closer to success.

Don't vacation on Someday Isle. Do something to earn your success, beginning today!

Three Things You Can Do to Make the Do-Something Choice

1. Spend more time on action and less time on thinking about what you want to do. Those who take action usually fare much better than those who are swept along by whatever life brings.

2. Study successful people. What choices have they made to help them reach their level of success?

3. Keep learning. Read every day. The difference between the successful and the mediocre is that the successful never stop learning.

Monday Morning Discussion Questions

1. What prevents us from moving off Someday Isle?

2. What would happen in our organization if every person decided to get serious about reading and committed to reading one book a month?

3. Name three things you have observed that the most successful people within your organization consistently do differently from everyone else.

Words of Wisdom about the
Do-Something Choice

If you think you're too small to have an impact, try going to bed with a mosquito in the room.

DAME ANITA RODDICK

Opportunities multiply as they are seized.

JOHN WICKER

Having the world's best idea will do you no good unless you act on it. People who want milk shouldn't sit on a stool in the middle of a field in hopes that a cow will back up to them.

CURTIS GRANT

Everyone who has ever taken a shower has an idea. It's the person who gets out of the shower, dries off, and does something about it who makes a difference.

NOLAN BUSHNELL

Decision is a sharp knife that cuts clean and straight. Indecision is a dull one that hacks and tears and leaves ragged edges behind.

JAN MCKEITHEN

Waiting is a trap. There will always be reasons to wait . . . The truth is, there are only two things in life, reasons and results, and reasons simply don't count.

ROBERT ANTHONY

One of the marks of successful people is that they are action-oriented. One of the marks of average people is that they are talk-oriented.

BRIAN TRACY

You can't build a reputation on what you are going to do.

HENRY FORD

Even if you're on the right track, you'll get run over if you just sit there.

WILL ROGERS

Monday Morning Choice #6

The Persistence Choice
. . . Learn from Failure

Many of life's failures are people who did not realize
how close they were to success when they gave up.
THOMAS EDISON

A memorable speech by a successful businessman was introduced by a wise master of ceremonies who announced: "Our man of the hour spent many days and nights getting there."

There is no such thing as instant success. Success is not an overnight accomplishment. It is the reward for persistence, sticking to it, and learning from failure.

Don't be surprised by what can happen in your life if you have the courage to persevere.

What Is Courage?

The dictionary tells us the word "courage" comes from the French word *coeur,* which means "heart." Courage is "the attitude of facing and dealing with anything recognized as dangerous, difficult, or painful instead of withdrawing from it." The second definition of "courage" is "the quality of being fearless or brave."

As early as the sixth century BC, ancient Greeks identified certain traits allowing common people to rise above the crowd. One of those traits—a characteristic vital to great long-term accomplishment—is persistence.

The slave Aesop described persistence in his ancient fable about a race between a slow tortoise and a swift hare. Halfway through the race, the hare was so far ahead and so confident of victory that he took a nap. The tortoise, not nearly as swift, continued plodding along, eventually passing the hare, who awoke just in time to see his slow-moving opponent cross the finish line.

Clearly the hare was faster and more athletic and should have won the race handily. However, his lack of persistence caused him to lose.

How often have we seen others with huge talents and great abilities end up going nowhere while many average men and women achieve greatness? Remember the girl or guy in your high school graduating class who was voted most likely to succeed? And then, at your class reunion, you learned that that girl or guy never achieved anything close to her or his potential?

Most of the time, the difference has been the choice to persist, to stick to it long enough to win.

The choice of persistence is about setting a goal and reaching it, about coming to roadblocks and hurdling them, about continuing the journey in spite of life's speed bumps. Most of the time, success will be achieved by those who want it most and will persevere past their failures.

The Courage to Persevere

The relationship between courage and fear is an interesting one. For some, courage means not feeling fear at all. Some suggest that men, in particular, interpret it this way. Sometimes people raise their children to think they shouldn't feel fear at all, that there is something wrong with them if they do. And fear of failure may prevent people from trying to succeed at all.

I don't buy that theory. I think it's okay to be afraid, because fear is a natural emotion experienced by everyone at one time or another. Fear, however, does not replace courage. Courage replaces fear.

"Courage," said Mark Twain, is "resistance to fear, mastery of fear—not absence of fear."

To complete our dictionary drill, what is the opposite of courage? Many say it is cowardice. Others say it is fear. Still others, ignorance.

Although any of those answers could apply, I think the most appropriate answer is conformity. Courage is having the guts, nerve, and heart to do things differently and allow progress to develop. Improvement does not happen by taking the path of least resistance and conforming to the way things always have been.

Courage is moving forward—even through the path of most resistance!

Hang in There Long Enough to Win

When I began my business, success did not come easily or quickly. My two partners had moved on when things got tough and did not go according to the business plan. Things were really tough. I was within weeks of giving up and returning to the more traditional corporate world.

Then, out of the blue, I was provided a way to sustain, grow, and prosper. As I was pondering my next career move I received a call from a business acquaintance, Mark Layton. I had known Mark during my time at FedEx. We were not particularly close—in fact, I had not seen him in years. Today he is my close friend and mentor.

His call came at a time when I was financially broke. Mark asked me to speak at a conference his company was sponsoring in Washington, D.C. I agreed, thinking this might be my last chance to represent CornerStone. Little did I know this was to be a defining moment for my company.

After the conference, Mark and I had several meetings that resulted in my training all of Mark's managers worldwide, sustaining my business long enough to gain the traction it needed to move forward.

If I had created a list of a hundred people I thought

might have that kind of impact on my life and business, Mark Layton might not have made my list. However, I believe that divine intervention occurred at that time and place in my life.

Many people quit right before they cross the finish line. Paul Harvey said that if there is one common denominator of men whom the world calls successful, it is this: "They get up when they fall down."

Your courage is ultimately measured by how much it takes to discourage you.

Make a Decision

There may be times when you have given it your best, the debts are high and the income is low, and you are faced with this decision: "Do I continue, or is it best to let go of the dream?" Only you can answer that question.

Ralph Waldo Emerson provided great advice for those at the crossroads of continuing or letting go of their dreams. He wrote in "Self-Reliance":

> *Trust thyself; every heart vibrates to that iron string. Accept the place the divine providence has found for you. . . . Nothing is at last sacred but the integrity of your own mind. . . . What I must do is all that concerns me, not what the people think. This rule, equally arduous in actual and in intellectual life, may serve for the whole distinction between greatness and meanness.*

If your answer is to stay the course, run the race! If your answer is to let go of the dream, have the courage to make that decision. Just don't straddle the fence.

Pass Go; Collect $200 or More!

Charles Parker loved playing games and included obstacles in many of the games he made up. While only a teenager he invented his first game, Banking, and at age sixteen, in 1883, he decided to publish it.

Turned down by two publishers, Parker was undaunted. When many would have given up and pursued other endeavors, he borrowed and saved until he had $40 to print five hundred sets of Banking. By the end of the year, he had sold all but twenty-four of the games, netting $100.

With his profits he started the George S. Parker Company, and after he had convinced his brothers, Charles and Edward, to join him, Parker Brothers was born.

By 1890, the company had twenty-nine games on the market, and when they introduced Monopoly in 1935, Parker Brothers had solidified its place as the game giant all over the world.

As with the strategy required to win in many of his games, Parker set an example that has taught us this lesson: you succeed only if you are persistent enough to stick to it long enough to win. Fortunately for almost all of us, Parker viewed his early failure as a healthy and inevitable part of the process on his way to success.

Failure Is Indeed an Option

After overcoming obstacles all of his life, Dr. Martin Luther King, Jr., also was convinced that "the measure of a man is not where he stands in moments of convenience, but where he stands in times of challenge and adversity."

In our society, "fail" has become an objectionable four-letter word, both personally and in business. We rarely use it, and most of us try not to think about it.

Young children learn early on that failing isn't acceptable behavior. In some cases, children are so frightened of failure that they often don't try new sports or accept new challenges. They have been conditioned to see failure as too harmful, too destructive, to be survived. Some people may be so afraid of failure that they never try to succeed.

In a recent sales meeting, clips from the popular movie *Apollo 13* were shown before the CEO of the company spoke to the sales force. Borrowing a phrase from the movie, the CEO tried to motivate his colleagues toward a record-breaking year by saying, "Failure is not an option."

Isn't it interesting, though, that success is usually preceded by failure? In fact, most successful people today find that their success is the result of persisting beyond failures. Usually not one failure but many failures enable them to discover their route to success.

Sticking to Failure

In 1968, 3M scientist Dr. Spencer Silver developed a new kind of glue, an unusual adhesive that formed tiny balls with the diameter of a paper fiber. These tiny spheres could not be melted and would not dissolve, but because these little balls made only intermittent contact, they didn't stick strongly. After several attempts to strengthen the adhesive, Dr. Silver set his glue aside as a useless failure.

Fast-forward to 1974, when fellow scientist Art Fry became frustrated one Sunday morning when his paper bookmark kept falling out of his hymnal as he sang in his church choir. Remembering Silver's failed adhesive, Fry went back to the lab, where he began working with the forgotten glue.

By coating the edge of a paper bookmark with this "failed" glue, Fry found that the coated paper would stay in place when needed, yet could be easily removed afterward without otherwise harming the page it was attached to.

It took another four years for Fry to convince higher-ups that his new product was valuable, and once he cleared that hurdle, the office supply distributors thought the product was a bad idea. They conducted market surveys, which also came back with negative responses.

Then, samples were mailed to secretaries of Fortune 500 CEOs, who found a multitude of uses for what they called sticky notes. Soon 3M began marketing them on a national scale.

By 1990, 3M's Post-it Notes were one of the five top-selling office-supply products in America.

Like these now familiar sticky slips of paper, most revolutionary products are built on failed prototypes that sent inventors back to the drawing board to make changes.

Learning from Failure

Henry Ford made many return trips to the drawing board as he developed his first automobiles and then began work on creating the first assembly line. "Failure is only an opportunity to more intelligently begin again," he assured the skeptics of his time.

The same is true for most technological devices. After a failure, designers review their objectives, make changes to overcome the obstacles they encountered with the last model, and eventually arrive at a successful conclusion. Inventor Thomas Edison knew this route well. "Some of the best lessons we ever learn we learn from our mistakes and failures," he said.

Successful people learn from failure. In fact, most successful people fail faster and more often than the average person. They learn enough from failure to become successful.

Success: The Tougher Choice

Without a doubt, it's always the easier choice to be satisfied with failure and give up. Aircraft designer Burt Rutan has had more than his share of failures, but those unsuccessful experiences did not cloud his vision.

Instead, he and his team of pilots and engineers continued reaching for their dreams of building, testing, and flying the first commercially viable manned spacecraft.

In October 2004, when the sleek *Spaceship One* poked through the cloudless horizon of the Mojave Desert, reaching an altitude of 368,000 feet above the Earth, Rutan and his team not only made way for commercial space flight but also won the coveted $10 million Ansari X Prize.

Awarded to the first privately funded commercial spacecraft to successfully complete two trips of at least 62.5 miles into space and return safely to Earth before January 2005, the Ansari X Prize was an incentive for jump-starting commercial space flight.

Obviously, it would have been much more comfortable for Rutan and his team to sidestep the risks required to continue after several hits and misses. However, to win, you have to stay in the game. The rewards far outweigh the pain of past failures for those who choose to overcome obstacles.

When failure comes, don't hang your head. Hold your head high so you can look failure squarely in the eye and say, "I am bigger than you. You cannot make me quit. I am going to learn from you and whip you."

Stick to it, and turn failure into success!

Three Things You Can Do to Make the Persistence Choice

1. When you reach roadblocks to your success, don't give up. Rarely does anyone succeed without overcoming obstacles.

2. Failure is a learning tool. Keep your eyes open to the opportunities that failure provides.

3. If you want to win, you have to stay in the game. Don't let temporary failure cause you to miss out on permanent success.

Monday Morning Discussion Questions

1. Was there a time when you were ready to quit right before a breakthrough that enabled you to continue and achieve greater results than you expected?

2. What was the most significant "failure" in your life, and how did you move beyond it?

3. Is there any such thing as permanent and absolute failure?

Words of Wisdom about the Persistence Choice

We must all suffer from one of two pains: the pain of discipline or the pain of regret. The difference is discipline weighs ounces while regret weighs tons.

JIM ROHN

If I had to select one quality, one personal characteristic that I regard as being most highly correlated with success, whatever the field, I would pick the trait of persistence. Determination. The will to endure to the end, to get knocked down seventy times and get up off the floor should be saying, "Here goes number seventy-one!"

RICHARD M. DEVOS

The credit belongs to the man who is actually in the arena; whose face is marred by dust and sweat and blood; who strives valiantly; who errs and comes short again and again; who knows the great enthusiasms, the great devotions, and spends himself in a worthy cause; who, at the best, knows in the end the triumph of high achievement; and who, at the worst, if he fails, at least fails while daring greatly, so that his place shall never be with those cold and timid souls who know neither victory nor defeat.

THEODORE ROOSEVELT

If you're willing to accept failure and learn from it, if you're willing to consider failure as a blessing in disguise and bounce back, you've got the potential of harnessing one of the most powerful success forces.

JOSEPH SUGARMAN

Never, never, never, never . . . give in.

WINSTON CHURCHILL

Mistakes are easy, mistakes are inevitable, but there is no mistake so great as the mistake of not going on.

WILLIAM BLAKE

Nothing in the world can take the place of persistence. Talent will not; nothing is more common than unsuccessful men with talent. Genius will not; unrewarded genius is almost a proverb. Education will not; the world is full of educated derelicts. Persistence, determination, and hard work make the difference.

CALVIN COOLIDGE

Success is not forever and failure isn't fatal.

DON SHULA

The Attitude Choice . . . Take the Enthusiastic Approach

There's very little difference in people. But that little difference
makes a big difference. The little difference is attitude.
The BIG DIFFERENCE is whether it is positive or negative.

W. CLEMENT STONE

A salesman moved into a new town and met an old-timer as he was leaving the bank. "I'm new to your town. What are the people like here?" the salesman asked.

"What were the people like in the town you came from?" the old-timer asked in return.

"Well, they were glum and negative and always complaining, and their glasses were always half empty, never half full," the salesman replied.

"Hmmm," said the old-timer. "Sounds about like the people who live here."

A few weeks later, another person moved to the same town and met the same old-timer as he was leaving the same bank. "I'm new to your town. What are the people like here?" the newcomer asked.

"What were the people like in the town you came from?" the old-timer asked again.

"Well, they were wonderful. They worked together in the neighborhood, helped each other out, and were always there to support us during tough times. We're going to miss them now that we've moved," the newcomer replied.

"Hmmm," said the old-timer. "I think you will like it here. That sounds about like the people who live here."

The old-timer's message? If you want to be around people who are positive and enthusiastic and eager to live life, your attitude has to be the same. If you think the people around you are glum and negative, you probably need to check your attitude. It's probably glum and negative, too.

If you want to be around happier people, choose to be happy yourself.

It all starts with you and your choice. As an old farmer used to tell his children, "You can't change the fruit without changing the root." Our root is our attitude, and our fruit is how others see us.

The longer we live and the older we get, the more evidence we have about how our attitude affects every aspect of our lives. If you look closely, you'll find that attitude becomes the linchpin for your opportunities, your circumstances, your successes, and your failures.

Whom would you rather spend time with?

A person who is cynical, pessimistic, sullen, and always looking for the sky to fall? Or would you rather be with a person who is optimistic and confident, who always looks for solutions and is enthusiastic about work and life?

If you are like most people, you probably chose the optimistic person. The fact is, we have an impact on everyone around us because of our own behavior.

An optimistic person is enthusiastic about life and those around him. The word "enthusiasm" comes from the Greek words *en theos*, meaning "God within." Enthusiasm is not something you put on or take off to fit the occasion—it is a way of life.

Is Attitude an Automatic Response?

Many people subscribe to the theory that attitudes are simply automatic responses to circumstances, that our attitude is simply a reflection of what's going on around us. The automatic response to something negative is usually negative, and the automatic response to something positive is usually positive. Whatever happens to us dictates the way we respond.

I don't buy that theory. While our immediate response may be a reflection of an event, we control our forward movement.

Of course, not all things that happen to us are within

our control, but we do control how we respond to those events. We choose how we react, what we tell ourselves about what happens to us. No one can make that choice for us.

We don't live in a Pollyanna world, where only good things happen to good people. Far from it. We all have things happen that are unexpected and unpleasant, and we have to deal with those events.

The Power of Our Attitudes

We may not want to admit this responsibility, but the facts are clear: we are in charge of our attitudes and our happiness. The choice about the attitude we'll embrace is a choice we make every day and a choice we make many times a day.

Your attitude is powerful. The difference between a good employee and a great employee, a good father or a great father, a good salesman or a great salesman, and a good leader or a great leader often is one thing: their attitude.

When facing serious illnesses, doctors confirm that the difference between survivors and those who do not survive is often the individual patient's attitude. In sports, coaches say that the attitude of the team is a major portion of the game plan. In school, teachers see evidence every day that positive kids produce positive results. In business, a Gallup poll revealed that 90 percent of people say they are more productive when they are around positive people.

The impact a positive attitude has on your success is not just theory but a research-based fact.

Martin Seligman, a psychologist at the University of Pennsylvania, has proved that optimists are more successful than equally talented pessimists in business, education, sports, and politics.

In one experiment with Metropolitan Life, he developed a survey (the Seligman Attribution Style Questionnaire) to sort the optimists from the pessimists in the hiring of sales personnel. The performance of both groups was then monitored and tracked. The results were very revealing. Optimists outsold pessimists by 20 percent the first year and 50 percent the following year.

Optimism increases energy and helps teams focus on long-term goals. It is a contributing factor to your success as well as to the success of those around you.

Why Choose to Be Negative?

If positive attitudes make us happier, more productive, and more successful, why would anyone choose negativism and all the ramifications that come along with that choice?

Maybe some people choose to be negative because they don't realize they have the power to be positive, or perhaps they enjoy feeling sorry for themselves (remember Poor Gary in Chapter 1?).

I think it is because negative attitudes are a natural response, they're easier responses, and some people enjoy being negative! Being positive in the face of a negative event takes work. The naysayers and those comfortable with negative attitudes rationalize by saying they are being "realistic," which, in most cases, means refusing to even acknowledge the "just as realistic" positive response.

Successful people choose not to inflict the poison of negative attitudes on themselves.

The Force Multiplier

Most people love to be around people who are positive and enthusiastic, always looking for the best. They attract others like a magnet; they are the force multiplier. Positive and enthusiastic people add energy to those around them, while negative and cynical people zap energy from their co-workers and team projects.

When was the last time you knew a successful person whom people consistently described as negative and cynical? In my years of experience, I cannot name one successful person described as negative. Not one!

Coincidental? I don't think so. Optimism and enthusiasm are two traits you'll find in most top employees and leaders, regardless of industry, profession, or age.

Optimism and enthusiasm are contagious. It is like the flu. If you want to catch the flu, go where people have the flu. Anytime you want to catch something, go where it is already there. If you can't find it at your job, start it yourself by finding others who have it, and you can be the one to spread the optimism virus in your workplace.

Cultivating Enthusiasm

Successful people cultivate the habit of enthusiasm in the same way others cultivate the habit of waking early or exercising. It takes time, perseverance, planning, and commitment.

The power of enthusiasm is evidenced by the effect it has on other people. We've all witnessed the enthusiastic schoolkids selling candy door to door. They are enthusiastic because they are confident in themselves, love their product (who doesn't love candy?), and enjoy achieving a goal. We're happy to buy from them.

We've also witnessed kids who are just trying to sell candy because it's an assignment, something they have to do. There is no passion, enthusiasm, or energy. The candy is the same, the customer is the same, but the sales are not even close. The missing ingredient is enthusiasm.

Real enthusiasm and a positive attitude are not traits you put on or take off to fit the occasion or to impress people. Real enthusiasm is a way of life. Yet, many people allow conditions to control their attitude rather than allowing their attitude to help control conditions.

Enjoying the Opportunity to Succeed

Here's the good news. We have an opportunity to choose our attitude for each situation every day, whether it is a change in job assignments, the way we spend our lunch hour, or our attitude while we're driving to work each day.

Truitt Brinson began his career in insurance sales by repeating "Today is my day of opportunity" every day before going to his office. He repeated it so often that his children were soon chanting the same daily mantra and grew to use it in their own lives.

Several years later, he recalled the practice as he accepted Mutual of New York's coveted Man of the Year award. "It's all about attitude," he said, "and my attitude is that I enjoy the opportunities I've been given to succeed every day."

All too often we may want to blame our attitude on past events and experiences in our lives.

Author Charles Dickens once advised, "Reflect upon your present blessings, of which every man has many—not on your past misfortunes, of which all men have some."

Dickens reminds us not to brood over mistakes, carry grudges, or harbor hate. Each of those negative emotions possesses the power to prevent us from accomplishing the successes we desire and deserve.

Expect Challenges

It is easy to have a positive attitude when things are going well. Unfortunately, life includes those times when things don't work the way we plan. When challenges emerge in your path, the best approach is to focus on what you desire, not what you fear. Allow your attitude to work for you by visualizing, believing, and taking action. Visualize future successes, believe you will achieve them and then move forward toward your goal.

When you invest yourself in working toward a goal, there is no time to think about the hurdles. Just keep moving.

Do you think your past has created a naturally negative attitude? Unfortunately, we cannot change our past or the fact that people act in a certain way. Remember, your attitude is not externally controlled. It is INTERNALLY controlled. If you have a negative attitude, it's because you've made the choice to have that negative attitude.

Opportunity or Calamity

Winston Churchill once said, "An optimist sees an opportunity in every calamity. A pessimist sees a calamity in every opportunity."

There is an enduring story that illustrates Churchill's point. Two researchers working for a large shoe manufacturer were independently dispatched to one of the world's least developed countries. Their task was to evaluate the business potential within that country.

After several weeks, the first report came back to the manufacturer's headquarters. The message read, "No market here. Nobody wears shoes." A few days later, the second report came back from the other researcher. It read, "Great market here. Nobody wears shoes!" Optimists see opportunity. Pessimists are blind to opportunity.

Fortunately, optimism can be learned and developed. Yes, you can choose how you react to events and challenges and become the architect of your own happiness.

Optimism Is a State of Mind

Optimism is a courageous state of mind. It comes from a person's desire, effort, and choice to accept and make the best of difficult situations. Certainly, the road of optimism is not without potholes, regardless of one's title or organization.

All of us will undoubtedly face setbacks and unexpected events that have the potential to be devastating. Things happen that shove us onto unfamiliar paths, testing even those with the most positive attitudes. Our challenge is to remember that negative events are a temporary setback.

It is easy to be optimistic when things are going well. However, the most successful people remain optimistic and search for the best, even in times of stress and uncertainty. No one enjoys the unknown, but regardless of the temporary struggle, those with positive attitudes keep focused on the best possible outcome.

Differences between Optimistic and Pessimistic People

An optimist looks for potential opportunities within difficulties.

An optimist sees setbacks as temporary and minor.

An optimist chooses to energize others and find creative solutions.

An optimist feels that he or she has sufficient control to make things happen.

An optimist sees the doughnut.

A pessimist sees only problems and makes difficulties of opportunities.

A pessimist chooses to see setbacks as permanent and catastrophic.

A pessimist zaps energy and destroys others' confidence.

A pessimist feels that everybody except himself or herself is in control.

A pessimist sees the hole.

Eyes-Wide-Open Attitude

About a century ago, among Atlanta pharmacist John Pemberton's inventions were hair dye, cough syrup, and liver pills. He had been working on a new invention—a headache syrup—but just couldn't seem to get it right.

One day he went to a back room of his pharmacy to discover two of his young employees mixing his new headache syrup with water and drinking it because, as they explained, they liked the taste.

Rather than becoming angry at his workers for loafing on the job, Pemberton chose to be curious about their claim and tried the remedy himself. *Not bad*, he thought as he added a little club soda to give the drink some fizz. "Even better," he pronounced.

Pemberton saw potential in a situation that would have been frustrating or even infuriating to most of us.

Soon after, the pharmacist began selling his newfound drink in his soda fountain, calling it Coca-Cola.

Growing Optimism

Want to be a more optimistic person? You can find the path in the Six Laws of Growing Optimism:

- *You reap only what you sow.* If you've sown apple seeds, you'll get apples. Don't expect oaks from apple seeds. If you want to be more optimistic, sow seeds of optimism. Sow positive behaviors to reap positive results, and surround yourself with positive people.

- *You need to know where to sow.* Seeds sown on rocks will never bear fruit. Find fertile ground, and sow your seeds there. Commit to positive projects, people, and tasks. Spend your energies to achieve positive goals, never wasting precious resources.

- *At some point, you must reap your harvest.* One farmer loved to cultivate and till the soil into neat rows and then sow his seed, but when it came time for harvest, he hated to drive the combine into the fields, crushing the neat mounds of soil and leaving nothing but chaff in its wake. If we sow, then we must reap. Otherwise, why bother?

- *You can't do anything about last year's harvest.* Life is filled with important choices, and every choice has a consequence. It's not about whether last year's harvest was good or bad. It's about how you handled the success or failure of that harvest. Did your failure prevent you from sowing positive seeds today? You can do something only about this year's crop, but you can also take what you learned last year and make this year's harvest more bountiful.

- *Don't worry about the weather, the beetles, or anything else.* Worrying is a wasted effort and a fertile breeding ground for self-doubt. It will lead you to focus on potential losses rather than effective solutions. Your best choice to stop worry is positive action.

- *Be easy on yourself.* It's important to have the strength and the desire to continue sowing. Beating yourself up for a poor harvest only wastes time. You can never like anyone more than you like yourself, and you can't expect others to like you if you don't hold yourself in high esteem.

The Lifesaving Value of Optimism

Max was always optimistic and a natural motivator, one of the principal reasons why he was successful in retail. Every day was a good day for business. His clerks liked what they saw in Max and emulated his approach to life. He was not only their hero but also successful in his career.

Early one morning, a robber made his way into Max's office, demanding that the manager lie down on the floor and give him the combination to the safe. After taking the money, the thief shot Max so he couldn't identify his assailant.

Luckily, Max was found soon afterward and was rushed to the hospital. After he had recovered, Max was asked whether he was afraid at any time in the aftermath of the shooting.

"Everyone was great," Max recalled. "But when I arrived in the emergency room, I could see that the doctors and nurses thought I was a goner, which is when I made the biggest choice of my life.

"A big burly nurse was shouting questions at me," Max remembered. "Then she asked whether I was allergic to anything. 'Yes,' I replied, and the medical team stopped working, waiting for more information. So I took a deep breath and yelled, 'Bullets!' Then, while they were still laughing, I added, 'And I am choosing to live, so see what you can do.'"

Yes, attitude is definitely a choice. It's the right choice for those who seek a successful career. Being optimistic will give you all the strength you need to keep moving successfully toward your goals.

Act It!

A positive attitude is more important to our success than how we dress, how we look, how much skill we have, how many degrees we've accumulated or how gifted we think we are.

You may say that optimism and enthusiasm do not come naturally to you. That is okay. Act it. If you assume a trait, you will later possess it naturally. If you act enthusiastic, you will be enthusiastic. You take hold of it, and it will take hold of you. Your positive enthusiasm will become a way of life.

Three Things You Can Do to Make the Attitude Choice

1. Consciously choose your attitude. Successful people cultivate a habit of positive enthusiasm.
2. Keep your eyes open to new opportunities— even when they come from the most unexpected places. Enjoy the opportunity to succeed.
3. Be easy on yourself and everyone else. We are all works in progress.

Monday Morning Discussion Questions

1. What if everyone imitated our attitude? What impact would that have on the organization?

2. Can you name a person you respect who has a negative, cynical attitude about work and life?

3. What actions can we take to create a more positive attitude within our organization?

Words of Wisdom about the Attitude Choice

Wake up with a smile and go after life . . . Live it, enjoy it, taste it, smell it, feel it.

JOE KNAPP

Think enthusiastically about everything; but especially about your job. If you do so, you'll put a touch of glory in your life. If you love your job with enthusiasm, you'll shake it to pieces.

NORMAN VINCENT PEALE

If you want to be happy, put your effort into controlling the sail, not the wind.

ANONYMOUS

Use words to change your situation, not to describe it.

LEE J. COLAN

Life is too short not to be happy and too long not to do well.

BRYAN DODGE

An obvious fact about negative feelings is often overlooked. They are caused by us, not by exterior happenings. An outside event presents the challenge, but we react to it. So we must attend to the way we take things, not to the things themselves.

VERNON HOWARD

Flaming enthusiasm, backed by horse sense and persistence, is the quality that most frequently makes for success.

DALE CARNEGIE

Surround yourself with people who are optimistic and caring; it's one time when being "surrounded" is a good thing.

AL LUCIA

Virtually nothing on earth can stop a person with a positive attitude who has his goal clearly in sight.

DENNIS WAITLEY

A happy person is not a person in a certain set of circumstances, but rather a person with a certain set of attitudes.

HUGH DOWNS

The Adversity Choice . . . Conquer Difficult Times

Within all of us are wells of thought and dynamos of energy which are not suspected until emergencies arise. Then, oftentimes, we find that it is comparatively simple to double or triple our former capacities and to amaze ourselves by the results achieved.

THOMAS J. WATSON

As we go through life the truest measure of our inner strength will be exposed when we are confronted by adversity. My greatest personal adversity challenge occurred several years ago. Within a span of six months, my wife, Karen, was diagnosed with a rare, aggressive cancer; my father passed away; and I had open-heart surgery.

Karen's doctors were hopeful for her recovery but not overly so. Ours would be a long road, and it wouldn't be easy. There would be chemo, surgery, more chemo, radiation, and possibly more surgery.

A few months after Karen was stabilized, my father had a heart attack and died.

After my father's death, I thought I might need to go to the doctor and get checked out. Admittedly, I had been under more stress than usual, but I felt I would pass all the tests with the usual flying colors. Of course, with Karen's illness and attending to the details that followed my father's death, I was more fatigued than usual, but I still had a full calendar of speeches and workshops to present, including one the next week in Cleveland.

The doctor's decision to admit me to the hospital for further tests the next morning, followed by preparation for quadruple bypass surgery, came as a big shock.

The pressure of facing those three major events almost simultaneously was almost too much to bear. However, through all those challenges I personally learned that adversity reveals how strong we really are.

Karen is now an inspiration for many others battling cancer. My dad—my mentor and guide—lived a full, wonderful life without suffering, and I have learned to focus my life on what is important!

No One Is Immune

In a recent meeting of twenty highly successful people, the topic of adversity was discussed. Every person there agreed that overcoming adversity was a critical turning point in their own personal success. But not until all participants began sharing the adversity they had personally overcome did I realize how universal adversity is.

Within that group, people had faced cancer, suicide, divorce, loss of children, drug abuse, loss of spouse, bankruptcy, and other major areas of struggle. Everyone there had faced a major crisis.

Wouldn't it be great if every morning when we woke up, all the issues that existed the previous day were gone? Life rarely works that way. Adversity is a part of life, and all of us will face challenges that test our ability to endure, continue, and survive. There is nothing like adversity to reveal how strong we really are.

Successful people have problems just like everyone else. Some adversities are beyond our control, while others are self-inflicted. But, regardless of how the adversity arrives, every successful person has faced, attacked, and conquered adversity somewhere along the way.

When adversity invades our lives, we soon discover what we are made of and what lies at the core of our character. To survive and to continue living full and rewarding lives, we must know how to effectively react to personal adversity as well as to the adversity that happens within our organization.

Mired or Motivated?

The difference between successful people and average people is that successful people make a conscious choice to spend their energy attacking the problem and moving forward.

Average people choose to spend their energy complaining, justifying, and blaming others for the problem. Perhaps you've found that this strategy doesn't help anyone. In fact, complaining drains the energy needed to begin working through the adversity.

Everyone faces adversity. No one is immune. Our gut check comes when things go wrong—an unexpected event that hits us squarely between the eyes.

After the shock of an unexpected event, we have to make a choice. We can choose to become mired in the quicksand of self-pity—immobilized, stuck, and unable to move ahead. Or we can make the choice to do what is necessary to attack and overcome adversity.

Look Around—There Are Plenty of Examples Close to You

If asked for examples of people who have attacked and overcome adversity, many would probably mention Lance Armstrong or Christopher Reeve. Both are great role models because they chose to avoid the muck of self-pity and to go on with life, becoming a voice for many others who were facing similar crises.

But look around your organization or circle of friends.

You probably don't have to look far to find examples of people who have chosen to attack and conquer personal adversity. They may not get the national attention, money, or resources like Armstrong or Reeve, but their challenges are just as dramatic.

One of the most positive and enthusiastic people I know is a friend named Melissa. When you meet Melissa, she appears to have it all: a terrific personality, good looks. She's smart, fun, and successful.

What is not apparent is that Melissa has survived and conquered major adversity that would have destroyed most people. Eight years ago, Melissa was a homemaker, taking care of her three-year-old autistic child and a newborn—a challenging full-time job, to say the least.

Then, one day without warning, Melissa's life suddenly changed. Without any explanation, her husband walked in and said he was leaving. He walked out the door and never turned back, leaving Melissa and the children with the house and the bills while he moved in with one of Melissa's good friends.

Melissa's world was shattered. Losing her husband and her friend and being left to pick up the pieces without financial or emotional support was enough to handle. On top of that, she did not have a job because she had left a bright and promising career four years earlier so she could stay home and have a family.

The most logical and easiest choice would have been for Melissa to become mired in self-pity, bitterness, and hatred over the unfair situation that had shattered her world—and who would blame her?

Some say adversity grinds you down. Others say it polishes you up. It depends on what you're made of and how you choose to attack the adversity that comes your way. Adversity polished Melissa up.

She chose to pick up the shattered pieces, one at a time, and continue to move forward with her life. The trip has not been easy, but she would not allow adversity to destroy her, her children, or their collective dreams.

Today, Melissa is a successful graphic designer for CornerStone Leadership Institute and is a tremendous inspiration to me.

Melissa chose to do the best she could with an unfair situation. Choice is power. When confronted with adversity, we can choose to see the positive alternatives and rise from the ashes to become even better and stronger than we were before.

Conquering Adversity

Chris Novak, my friend and author of *Conquering Adversity*, a book I think every person walking this earth needs to read, is a great example of making the choice to move forward, even after unimaginable tragedy.

Chris, a happily married family man with one child and another on the way, received a phone call in the middle of just another day at the office, saying his wife and unborn son had been killed in an automobile accident. That call would change his life forever. No one would have blamed him for being bitter and consumed with the unfairness of life.

Yet, after grieving this tragic loss, Novak chose to take the lessons of catastrophe and create opportunities from the alternatives his life now offered.

In *Conquering Adversity* he tells how he was able to move forward, saying, "Life is not fair, so don't expect it to be. Regardless of how bleak the situation appears, there are alternatives that will help you move forward . . . if you choose to see them."

Chris Novak suggests that you attack adversity by doing the following:

- *Affirmation.* Acknowledge what is and what is not lost. It is natural in times of extreme duress to believe that everything is lost. But even in the greatest of tragedies, we have to acknowledge that we do not lose everything. The fear of moving forward is the power adversity has over us. Ultimately, we have to make the decision to move ahead.

- *Expectation.* Adversity attacks our vision, limits our sight, and blinds us with the challenges of the moment. After adversity attacks us, we have to make the choice to pull ourselves up, avoid the "why" trap, and move forward with positive expectations.

- *Communication.* To conquer adversity, we have to allow others to help. Many times we struggle by ourselves, dealing with adversity when someone just a phone call away will have an answer that can move us forward. People want to help, but most of the time they have to be invited.

- *Locomotion.* One of the greatest dangers in facing adversity is that we panic, freeze, and stop because we perceive the roadblocks, barriers, or mountains in our lives as insurmountable. People respond better to crisis when they maximize their forward motion. We have to keep moving forward.

- *Collaboration.* Most challenges we face cannot be overcome alone. We should not attempt to meet adversity with no one to support us. Collaboration is about the people we take with us on our journey forward.

- *Celebration.* Celebration feeds our positive energy and our sense of hope. It nourishes our spirits, refreshes our attitudes, and gives us strength to fight off the inevitable attacks of negativism and fear that accompany severe adversity.

Today, Chris Novak continues to live his life to its fullest. He has remarried and is enjoying seeing his son grow into adulthood. His metamorphosis serves as an exquisite model for all of us about how to use catastrophe as a catalyst in our lives. Chris is the perfect example of attesting that there are

alternatives, even in life's most painful shadows, but he is also
the first to admit that the options for his life became suddenly
more plentiful as he began to know himself within the con-
text of his devastating loss.

Explore Your Alternatives

Without question, the better we know ourselves, the more
alternatives we can see for our future. Our personal store of
energy, along with our time, is our most valuable commodity.
In the face of adversity, we must ask ourselves, "How can my
time and energy best be used in this situation right now?"

The obvious answer is this: "Use your energy to explore
workable alternatives—so you can move to the next level."

It is our role to clear a path to success by overcoming
adversity. Whatever adversity you are facing, personally or
professionally, it's important to realize that you are not the
first person to face your problem. Other people have overcome the same challenge or one similar to the situation that
is consuming your thoughts, energy, and hopes. Remember,
from the moment you embark on your journey to overcome
adversity, people will help you if you ask them to help.

Three Things You Can Do to Make the Adversity Choice

1. Realize that adversity is short term. Allow others to help you work your way through the adversity you are facing.

2. Don't panic, freeze, and stop because you perceive the adversity as insurmountable. You can respond better to crisis when you maximize your forward motion. Keep moving forward.

3. Don't waste your energy looking for someone to blame. Choose to see the positives and opportunities to grow, even in the face of adversity.

Monday Morning Discussion Questions

1. Can you give an example of when adversity attacked and ultimately turned out to be a blessing in disguise?

2. How can we help those within our organization who are going through adversity right now?

3. How can we use Chris Novak's six-step process to work through adversity within our organization?

Words of Wisdom about the
Adversity Choice

The very greatest things—great thoughts, discoveries, inventions—have usually been nurtured in hardship, often pondered over in sorrow, and at length established with difficulty.

SAMUEL SMILES

This, too, shall pass.

WILLIAM SHAKESPEARE

We must look for the opportunity in every difficulty instead of being paralyzed at the thought of the difficulty in every opportunity.

WALTER E. COLE

The measure of a man is not where he stands in moments of convenience, but where he stands in times of challenge and adversity.

DR. MARTIN LUTHER KING, JR.

Adversity causes some men to break, others to break records.

WILLIAM ARTHUR WARD

Tackling adversity means moving forward with the knowledge that some questions need action, not answers.

CHRIS NOVAK

If things go wrong, don't go with them.

ROGER BABSON

Every winner has scars.

HERBERT CASSON

*Things don't go wrong and break your heart so you can be-
come bitter and give up. They happen to break you down
and build you up so you can be all that you were intended
to be.*

CHARLIE "TREMENDOUS" JONES

*Character cannot be developed in ease and quiet. Only
through experiences of trial and suffering can the soul be
strengthened, vision cleared, ambition inspired, and success
achieved.*

HELEN KELLER

Part III

Investment Choices: Making Your Success Lasting and Meaningful

Make every thought, every fact, that comes into your mind pay you a profit. Make it work and produce for you. Think of things not as they are but as they might be. Don't merely dream—but create!

ROBERT COLLIER

The Relationship Choice
. . . Connect with Success

Personal relationships are the fertile soil from which all
advancement, all success, all achievement in real life grows.
BEN STEIN

H ave you ever wondered how bees survive the winter?
Interestingly, they survive because of mutual aid and unselfish teamwork. When winter arrives, the bees form into a ball. All the bees—even the ones on the outside of the ball—move continually. Their movement is like chaotic dancing.

After a while, the bees change places. The bees in the center of the ball rotate to the outside of the ball, and all the other bees move inward. They all have to sacrifice and move to the outside of the ball and then await their chance to return to the center. To survive the winter, they must work together as a team.

If the bees in the center were to decide not to rotate, the entire hive would eventually die. Even the ones in the temporary warmth of the center would die.

Just as the bees cannot survive without the others, no one can achieve long-term success alone. Everyone needs other people's help!

Building Relationships

Our relationships, from close family members to co-workers, from bosses to employees, often decide our direction and are an important part of our lives. No one can achieve long-term success working alone on his or her own personal island. Why? The ability to develop trust and get along with others is a basic requirement for success.

A Carnegie Foundation study once showed that only 15 percent of success could be attributed to job knowledge and technical skills. Of course, you need knowledge and skills. However, this will not be the primary determinant of your success. The Carnegie study showed that 85 percent of a person's success is determined by what the researchers called ability to deal with people and attitude.

Some of us may have a vast circle of relationships. Others may prefer a more intimate group. Yet, the skills in building and maintaining these relationships are shared across the spectrum.

But how do we learn to build these relationships? Who teaches us how to develop positive relationships with others?

We may have role models within our families or a mentor at school or at work. An older brother or sister may help us pattern our relationships, or perhaps we take our cues from a relative whom we admire and try to emulate. We may model a person down the hall in the office or someone whom we have admired from afar.

Many of us, however, go it alone, relying on our own instincts when we create our own models for building relationships. We take advice from teachers, books, influential associates, or larger-than-life heroes on the sports field or the movie screen. Then we put them all together in an enormous collage and use it as a guide for forming and nurturing our relationships.

There is no set pattern for relationships. There are no universal criteria. Each individual desires and seeks something slightly different in a relationship from everyone else.

No matter where your ideas about relationships have come from, sooner or later you will discover that relationships are a requirement for success. You cannot achieve success alone.

But relationships don't just happen. Healthy, wholesome, energizing relationships take time and energy from both people involved, and these healthy relationships have a tendency to grow and change over time.

Developing Stable Relationships

Researchers have found that the basis for any healthy relationship is trust. Individuals within healthy relationships also have a willingness to talk through problems, to share openly, and to develop a comfortable way to share positive and negative feelings with each other.

Individuals in healthy relationships also

- Are interested in the feelings, concerns, and dreams of others.

- Are willing to take responsibility for improving the relationship and encourage other people to do the same.

- Know that relationships are about more than "what's in it for me?" and are also about what they can bring to the relationships.

- Understand that other people not only bring good to experiences but also, perhaps, bring some negative baggage from other relationships.

- Know that their actions affect other people's happiness and success.

Strangely, in our twenty-first-century society, when we mention "relationships," most people assume we're talking about a romantic bond between two people.

In reality, we probably spend less time with our romantic partners than we do with other people, and we may even spend less time and effort building that romantic relationship than we spend building relationships in the workplace or in other areas of our life.

Strong, positive relationships don't just happen. A pre-relationship bonding may occur. We may find that perfect chemistry between mentor and student, or have an "aha" experience with that individual who shares many of our same interests, but a strong relationship requires time, attention, understanding, and a willingness to perceive the needs of the other person to be as important as our own.

It is also true that relationships are sometimes exploited, damaged, or forgotten. Others simply run their course, ending abruptly when one of the individuals meets with hardship. This often happens when fair-weather friendships are formed solely because of the "what's in it for me" motivation.

A Bear's Advice on Relationships

As the ancient Aesop recalled, two friends were traveling in the woods when a large, hungry bear appeared down the trail. As the bear approached, one of the friends climbed high up into a tree and hid, not offering to help his companion scale the tree. Left with few alternatives, the second friend, who was not as nimble, threw himself on the ground and pretended to be dead, as he had heard that bears would not touch a dead body.

The bear sniffed all around the man on the ground, took him to be dead, and went away.

As soon as it was safe, the man came down from the tree and asked his friend what the bear had whispered when he put his mouth to his friend's ear. "He told me to never again travel with a friend who deserts you at the first sign of danger," the survivor replied.

Choosing the Right Relationships

One of our most important choices is whom we hang around with. Eventually, we become like the five people we hang around with the most, which could be a blessing or a curse. Be careful who you choose as your closest associates.

Be careful in whom you invest your time. Being around people who are like a swamp—with bloodsucking mosquitoes, diseases, alligators, and snakes—will drain you and prevent you from achieving your goals.

Improving Relationships

Whether the relationship is with your partner, boss, coworkers, or friends, there's always room for improvement, so cement those important interactions with more effort on your part. Here are five steps to help cement relationships:

- Your relationships reflect the relationship you have with yourself. Remember the old saying, "You have to be a friend before you can make friends." So step one is finding peace within yourself. Nobody but you can make you happy. It is futile to look elsewhere to find happiness. Treat yourself with caring acceptance and gentle compassion.

- People want to know that you care about them. Show them you care. Take a backward glance and think of those who have made you feel special. In most cases, those people made it obvious that they cared about you. No relationship can strengthen and grow in an environment of negativity. Positive thoughts and deeds inspire other people's respect and cause them to value their relationships with you.

- We all have busy schedules, but you cannot have a relationship without taking the time to make contact and nurture the relationship. Positive relationships require dedicated time. Take the time necessary to let the people most important in your life know that you have time for them.

- Conflicts will occur in any relationship. Be willing to compromise rather than focusing on winning or losing an argument. The ultimate test of a relationship is to disagree but to respect the other person, acknowledge your agreement to disagree, and move forward without bitterness.

- Practice forgiveness when the relationship is tested. Forgiveness is the "oil" of relationships.

Be patient, and allow time for you and the other person to grow.

Want to expand your circle, increasing your opportunities to build new relationships? There are countless opportunities to meet new people, network, and form new relationships. Look around. There are probably numerous people within your work group whom you know nothing about. The loss is yours.

Don't know how to network? Here are a few tips:

Decide your interests and join new groups. Get involved. Joining without being involved will not help you develop relationships.

Stick around. Most relationships are developed either before or after the meeting. Work the room and meet as many people as you can.

Pay attention. If you know people in the group, be sure to ask how projects, event planning, committees, or family activities are going.

If you say you'll get back with someone or want to follow up, do it.

Become a mentor for others. Deep relationships are formed when you share the experiences that made you who you are today. People need your counsel, advice, and wisdom, so don't keep it to yourself.

Social researchers have found that healthy relationships are a necessity for success. Relationships provide someone to share with, someone to learn from, someone to talk to, and someone to confide in. They offer understanding when we fail, solace when we grieve, and celebration when we continue with our lives.

Relationships are pivotal interactions in enjoying all life has to offer—and key to moving ahead toward success.

Three Things You Can Do to Make the Relationship Choice

1. Focus on building positive relationships with your peers, subordinates, friends, and boss. Invest time in recognizing your professional relationships. Everyone has a basic need to know that he or she is making a difference. For those making a difference in your life, take the time to write them a note and express your appreciation for their relationship.

2. Become a mentor for others. People need your counsel, advice, and wisdom, so don't keep it to yourself.

3. Don't travel with friends who desert you at the first sign of danger.

Monday Morning Discussion Questions

1. What relationships have an impact on our success?

2. How much time do we invest in mentoring others through tough times?

3. What can we do to develop a positive relationship with all those around us?

Words of Wisdom about the Relationship Choice

Even the Lone Ranger didn't do it alone.

HARVEY MACKAY

When weighing the faults of others, be careful not to put your thumb on the scale.

UNKNOWN

When nobody around you seems to measure up, it's time to check your yardstick.

BILL LEMLEY

We become who we spend time with. The quality of a person's life is most often a direct reflection of the expectations of their peer group. Choose your friends well.

ANTHONY ROBBINS

I believe that you can get everything in life you want if you will just help enough other people get what they want.

ZIG ZIGLAR

You can make more friends in two months by becoming interested in other people than you can in two years by trying to get other people interested in you.

DALE CARNEGIE

Do not be misled: Bad company corrupts good character.

1 CORINTHIANS 15:33 (NIV)

One of the secrets of a long and fruitful life is to forgive everybody everything every night before going to bed.

BERNARD BARUCH

The most important thing in communication is to hear what isn't being said.

PETER F. DRUCKER

The golden rule is of no use whatsoever unless you realize that it is your move.

DR. FRANK CRANE

Nice guys may appear to finish last, but usually they are running in a different race.

KEN BLANCHARD

There is no exercise better for the heart than reaching down and lifting people up.

JOHN ANDRES HOLMES

The Criticism Choice . . .
Embrace Tough Learning

Remember, if people talk behind your back,
it only means you're two steps ahead.
FANNIE FLAGG

When Ronald Reagan succeeded Edmund G. Brown as governor of California in 1967, Brown told him, "There is a passage in *War and Peace* that every new governor with a big majority should tack on his office wall."

In the passage, Count Rostov, after weeks as the toast of elegant farewell parties, gallops off on his first cavalry charge and finds real bullets snapping at his ears. "Why, they're shooting at me," he says. "Me, whom everyone loves!"

There's no escaping the fact—whether you're at the head of your class, at the top of your profession, or simply leading the charge—your success will inevitably breed criticism. The higher people go in their fields, the more susceptible they are to criticism, even if they feel that they, like Count Rostov, are loved by everyone and are doing everything right.

Ronald Reagan, then the governor and soon to be the fortieth president of the United States, never forgot the departing Brown's counsel. Leaders attract criticism, and yet this same criticism can be a reminder to rethink the most solid of positions.

During his two terms in office, Reagan's goal was to reinvigorate the American people. Many believe he accomplished this by dealing skillfully with Congress, obtaining legislation to stimulate economic growth, increase employment, and curb inflation. Often it was the criticism he received that helped him rethink his strategy and focus on the bigger picture.

It's Lonely at the Top

There's no escaping the fact that success breeds criticism. So what is criticism, really? It is generally thought of as disapproval or judgment that underscores faults or shortcomings, but I want you to think of criticism in a positive light, too.

You've probably never met anyone who didn't want to be liked, respected, and accepted. In a perfect world, we would expect everyone to agree with our ideas, and we would want our actions to be praised as the best ever. But the reality is that we will have critics, and having critics is good. Our choice is about what we do with criticism that comes our way.

From an early age, we are trained to be critical. Think about your first-grade teacher—the one who wanted you to write a little larger, the one who asked you to read a little louder in reading group, or the one who asked if you would just keep your hands to yourself on the way to the water fountain.

That was criticism. Very gentle, but firm, nonetheless. By the time we were in middle school, the criticism was coming not only from our teachers and parents but also from our peers and perhaps others who didn't even know us.

Successful people have a tendency to attract those who will criticize their every move. In one office I visited recently, it appeared to me as though the corporate culture included backstabbing and criticizing every single action.

It was like a game. The fast-trackers were criticized for everything, from their hairstyles to the way they had their offices arranged. It was as though the in-house critics were waiting for the fast-trackers' next moves so they would have something else to discuss critically. Any wonder why turnover was more than 40 percent in that organization?

That type of criticism—criticism focused on your person—will not help you become more successful. Those critics are not worth spending your time on to understand. Instead, look for the critics who can help you learn from your mistakes so you can achieve your goals.

One Old Bullfrog

One warning: don't overreact to criticism. While those who are critical may be vocal, they may be alone in their criticism.

There is a story about an old farmer who advertised his "frog farm" for sale. The farm, he claimed, had a pond filled to the brim with fine bullfrogs.

When a prospective buyer appeared, the old farmer asked him to return that evening so he might hear the frogs in full voice. When the buyer returned, he was favorably impressed by the symphony of magical melodies emanating from the pond, and he signed the bill of sale on the spot.

A few weeks later, the new owner decided to drain the pond so he could catch and market the plentiful supply of frogs—but to his amazement, when the water was drained from the pond, he found that all the noise had been made by one old bullfrog.

The same may also be said about criticism in an organization. Usually, the most noise is made by only one old bullfrog.

Choosing to Embrace Criticism

So why would we want to choose criticism? Don't we already have enough on our plates without having to make room for naysayers?

Ultimately, we all need criticism, no matter how successful we become. Criticism whips our fragmented attention into laser focus on some of the more important aspects of our jobs and our lives. Some call criticism a teaching tool. More specifically, it is a learning tool that teaches us hard lessons.

Contrary to what many people think, criticism isn't always negative. In fact, in many forums, criticism is a positive, necessary part of growth.

If we examine our own criticisms of others, we'll discover that we use our own narrow standards to judge others, from spouses to houses. Obviously, for criticism to be meaningful, the better path is to be more flexible and less judgmental when we look at others and their actions. Just because we wouldn't have done it the same way doesn't mean another's approach doesn't have merit—and perhaps more merit than our own approach.

The healthy approach to criticism is to pay attention to it. Always listen with the intent to understand why the criticism is being leveled at you and why the critic may want you to know his or her feelings.

You may not believe it, but there's an upside to criticism, too. Criticism from the right people could lead to improvement.

Many employees dread performance reviews. They know that criticism is on its way, even though there are probably more positives than negatives in performance reviews. The people who pay attention to the feedback and make adjustments based on it are the ones who will ultimately become the obvious choice for the next promotion.

The biggest room we have is room for improvement. There's always something we can do better, more often, or with a different intensity. Appropriate criticism helps us focus our attention on what we need to do to become more successful.

Avoiding Psychosclerosis

We've all heard people say, "I welcome constructive criticism," but sometimes that invitation is hard to believe.

Why? Because of our human nature, constructive criticism carries a certain sting, even though it may help us correct a wrong, strengthen a weakness, or chart a more successful course. One reason for criticism's stinging effect is something referred to as psychosclerosis: our natural human tendency to think our idea is the best—or the only—idea that will work.

The second phase of full-blown psychosclerosis is becoming closed-minded to any suggestion. So if we think we have the best or only idea and we're closed to any suggestions, the result is that we become stagnated in our own stubbornness.

The opposite of psychosclerosis is the ability to be flexible, listening with the intent to learn so we can make a better, more educated decision.

Once you make the "criticism choice," what's the best way to handle criticism from your colleagues, your boss, your friends or your partner? Here are a few suggestions:

- Acknowledge that criticism is a form of feedback, and we all need feedback.

- Ask yourself these questions: Who's offering the criticism, and are they qualified? Are they trying to hurt you, or help? Objectively, is there any truth to what they're saying?

- Constructive criticism is a gift. Thank the giver.

- Stay positive no matter what. Don't put your self-esteem at the mercy of others. Liking who you are makes it easier to evaluate the criticism of others.

- Attempt to transform criticism that seems directed at you personally to specific behavioral issues. Personal criticism may weaken one's resolve. Focus the criticism on your actions, not your person. Pay particularly close attention to criticism that addresses behaviors in a timely and specific manner.

- After you have had a chance to review the criticism, communicate clearly how you feel and think about it. Then take appropriate action to improve.

- If you want constructive criticism from others (and you should), be willing to return the favor if they are interested.

Moving Forward

Sometimes we become paralyzed by critics. They become so vocal and so loud that it's difficult to remember our mission and move forward.

In the midst of the Civil War, Abraham Lincoln was being criticized on all fronts—by citizens, advisors, politicians, military leaders. Everyone was telling him what he should do to win the war.

He is said to have remarked that he "felt like a man lost in a dense forest during a severe thunderstorm who prayed, 'Oh, Lord, if it's all the same to you, please give me more light and a little less noise.'"

Sometimes we simply need to listen to the criticism and understand it the best we can, but move forward!

Using Criticism

Criticism is a fact of life. You have the choice to perceive criticism as a hindrance or a help. Experts in human behavior encourage us to be prepared to accept criticism and to accept it graciously.

Realistically, criticism should eventually become a tool, helping us grow as individuals while we evolve our skills and our ideas. Ultimately, we can find the fine line between dismissing criticism and clinging to each word we hear. At this point, we will learn to welcome criticism rather than become defensive when criticism comes our way.

Three Things You Can Do to Make the Criticism Choice

1. Be aware that criticism comes with success. Embrace it and learn from it.
2. Accept constructive criticism as a gift. It can enlighten you to the changes you need to make to be successful.
3. Acknowledge that criticism is a learning tool that teaches you lessons throughout your life.

Monday Morning Discussion Questions

1. Why is our natural instinct to become defensive about criticism?

2. Can you name a time when the criticism you received was the catalyst to your success?

3. Is there a time when criticism can be correct but wrong?

Words of Wisdom about the Criticism Choice

The trouble with most of us is that we would rather be ruined by praise than saved by criticism.

NORMAN VINCENT PEALE

Criticism is the windows and chandeliers of art: it illuminates the enveloping darkness in which art might otherwise rest only vaguely discernible, and perhaps altogether unseen.

GEORGE JEAN NATHAN

We can't learn anything new until we can admit that we don't already know everything.

ERWIN G. HALL

Life asks us to make measurable progress in reasonable time. That's why they make those fourth grade chairs so small—so you won't fit in them at age twenty-five!

JIM ROHN

He that won't be counseled can't be helped.

BENJAMIN FRANKLIN

Listen to advice and accept instruction, and in the end you will be wise.

PROVERBS 19:20 (NIV)

Courage is what it takes to stand up and speak; courage is also what it takes to sit down and listen.

ANONYMOUS

The healthy and strong individual is the one who asks for help when he needs it. Whether he's got an abscess on his knee, or in his soul.

RONA BARRETT

He has the right to criticize who has the heart to help.

ABRAHAM LINCOLN

The Reality Choice . . .
Face the Truth

Don't paint stripes on your back if you're not a zebra.
Focus on building upon your unique abilities.
LEE J. COLAN

Carmen Silva had worked for years to reach her position as a manager for a large corporation. Yet, as she watched colleagues move ahead in their careers, the reality was that her own career was being slowed because of her long-standing fear about speaking in front of groups.

Nick Bagby made his quota every month. He had won every award for productivity and had even earned several trips to

Hawaii as leading sales rep for his division, but he had been passed over for sales manager promotions for the past three years. In his place, two colleagues had gone on to higher positions.

"Nothing personal, Nick," his boss had said, trying to reassure him. "The reality is that since your kids are in school, you've never wanted to relocate your family—and we haven't had openings here in over five years."

Carl Landon had been a top-notch office manager for a large corporation for several years, but he had always wanted to go into sales. However, every time he had approached the VP of sales about the possibilities of joining the sales force, he had been less than encouraged. Finally, he confronted the VP. "What's wrong with me becoming a sales rep?" he wanted to know.

"Frankly, Carl," the VP responded, "I just don't think that job is right for you. It requires a lot of self-motivation to succeed in sales, and, as we've discussed in the past, self-motivation is just not something you've demonstrated in your current assignment."

The reality: Carl had been "interviewing" all along. His skills and personality were better suited to a structured environment.

History chronicles our preference to avoid facing reality. In 1775, American patriot Patrick Henry spoke of this prefer-

ence to the Continental Congress about the British intent to
subjugate the colonies:

> *We are apt to shut our eyes against a painful truth,
> and listen to the song of that siren till she transforms us
> into beasts. . . . Are we disposed to be of the number of
> those who, having eyes, see not, and having ears, hear
> not, the things which so nearly concern their temporal
> salvation? For my part, whatever anguish of spirit it
> may cost, I am willing to know the whole truth; to
> know the worst, and to provide for it.*

All too often, when we suddenly find ourselves facing
reality, it's not a reality we want to see. We tend to think we
are objective—but in most cases we're not.

In Carl's case, as an example, he wanted to try his luck, to
see if he could perform as well as—or better than—the current sales reps. He thought he had the personality; he thought
he knew the products and their selling points.

All he needed was a chance, but the reality was that the
current VP wasn't too impressed with the way Carl handled
slack times, the times top sales reps spent developing leads and
making cold calls. Apparently the VP couldn't envision Carl
performing without a specific routine, one that had built-in
accountability at every turn. Carl failed to realize that he was
interviewing for his next opportunity while working his current job.

The Truth of Reality

A definition of the word "reality" tells us it is the real nature of something; the truth or something that is actual, not imaginary.

A key element to your success will be discovering and facing reality. The process of discovering reality includes examining the facts and separating them from feelings and egos.

"So why is the choice of reality necessary for a successful life journey?" you may be asking.

We choose reality and use it as a springboard to our next goal-setting process. We choose reality as a tool to understand what's in front of us, from the opportunities along our current path to the challenges that loom ahead.

Choosing reality provides us with a major indicator about where we are, where we're going, and what we have to do to get there.

It's like visiting a large mall and searching for the map of stores so we can locate the nearest coffee shop or optician: choosing reality tells us, "You are here." Then, when we use the map as a guide to where we want to go next, reality allows us to plot our path to get from where we are to where we want to go.

Choosing reality also helps us make those difficult decisions. When the VP of sales pointed out that Carl, the office manager who wanted to be a sales rep, didn't always use his slack time productively, reality provided Carl with three options: he could keep on being an office manager, he could learn to use his slack time wisely, or he could go to another company to make a fresh start.

Reality also can help us identify our limits. During the last several seasons of his career, former Dallas Cowboys quarterback Troy Aikman was warned by his doctors that repeated concussions had placed him in a precarious position every time he walked onto the playing field. He had the ability to continue to be a great quarterback, but it would take only one more crushing, jarring tackle to place his life in jeopardy. For Aikman, his personal reality became ominous: continuing his football career could cost him his life. He chose not to endanger his health by continuing to do something he loved and was great at. Instead, he moved into a field that was unknown to him. He's now a well-respected commentator for Fox Sports.

In business, the limits of reality can come in the form of our abilities, our product, our leadership, or even the capitalization of a company or the wishes of stockholders. During the past decade, the reality of downsizing meant that many in the workforce had to retool their skills and enter other industries.

The old phrase "time for a reality check" is exactly the approach workers should take in assessing where they are and where they want to be or where they want to go. Reality, for most of us, means change. Reality could also mean a change in our direction, a change in our approach to solving a problem, or a change in our team.

Stopping for a Reality Check

All too often, we don't stop long enough for a reality check and keep going as long as we can, until there are no other options. Like so many today, we're in such a hurry with such busy schedules that we don't take time to stop to refill the fuel tank until we're on the freeway at rush hour, praying we can make it to a gas station before our vehicle sputters to a stop.

Choosing reality can help us avoid those awkward moments, whether it's running out of fuel on the freeway or sitting across the desk during an exit interview with a favorite employee. Choosing reality can mean sizing up what it takes to clear the hurdle ahead of us before taking the next giant step in our careers or, like Troy Aikman, understanding that making changes now may be our best option.

But choosing reality does not mean abandoning lofty goals and dreams. In fact, it's just the opposite. Being realistic provides us with the best chance of attaining those dreams. Why? Because reality keeps giving accurate and objective assessments of what we need to reach success.

In 1994, a popular movie, *Reality Bites,* involved the realities of the lives of Gen-Xers as they made the transition from college to careers. The message carried by the title sums up the negative aspects of reality. Sure, reality "bites" when you suddenly find yourself in a job you don't like or when you discover you're working for a company that's struggling.

Reality "bites" when your partner no longer wants to share your life, when you can no longer afford a certain lifestyle, or when you find that your firstborn has been sneaking out of the house after you're asleep.

Yes, choosing reality can often lead you down a murky path where you may refuse to speak the unspeakable or think the unthinkable. But by choosing reality, you're taking the first step in solving the problem or ending a situation that is not only disturbing to you but also probably sapping your emotional energy.

Reality Rewards

Are there rewards for confronting these hard realities? Absolutely! Of course, you should prepare yourself to encounter frequent delays in your forward progress, as well as bouts of self-doubt and pessimism. However, by making the reality choice, not only are you rewarded by learning more about yourself, but also you will find that dealing with obstacle after obstacle enables you to use many of these challenges to your advantage.

In discussing the necessary traits of future business leaders, Harvard's Ronald Heifetz has said that "tomorrow's greatest leaders are those with the courage to face reality and help the people around them face reality." When they do so, the vision of that organization becomes accurate, and strategies can be developed to achieve what's possible within this authentic vision.

As you plot your plan for the next year or set your goals for the next five years, some of the realities you will assess are the skills, time, resources, and motivation needed to reach those goals, and whether there is a gap between these resources and what your goals demand for success.

Choosing reality takes courage. It takes strength of conviction and a passion for progress. All too often, we'd be much more comfortable kicking reality under the carpet as we stand and admire our last award-winning project.

But if we choose reality and all this choice entails, we will find the road to success a little straighter, the challenges less overwhelming, our goals within easier reach, and fewer surprises along the way.

Three Things You Can Do to Make the Reality Choice

1. A key element of your success is discovering and facing reality. Reality is actual, not imaginary. Make reality checks a daily habit.

2. Look for truth in every situation, every relationship, every crisis, and every success. Reality checks help you identify your limits and allow you to focus on your opportunities.

3. Understand that choosing reality may not always be the easiest path, but, bottom line, it will push you ahead on the road of life.

Monday Morning Discussion Questions:

1. Think of a situation in which you refused to choose reality. Were there any consequences—positive or negative—resulting from that choice?

2. What is a current reality for you? Are you choosing it or ignoring it? Why?

3. Has there ever been a reality for your team that you saw but were afraid to point out? What happened?

Words of Wisdom about the Reality Choice

Your big opportunity may be right where you are now.

NAPOLEON HILL

There is nothing so powerful as truth—and often nothing so strange.

DANIEL WEBSTER

Truth is not beautiful, neither is it ugly. Why should it be either? Truth is truth.

OWEN C. MIDDLETON

Accept everything about yourself—I mean everything. You are you and that is the beginning and the end—no apologies, no regrets.

CLARK MOUSTAKAS

No man, for any considerable period, can wear one face to himself, and another to the multitude, without finally getting bewildered as to which may be true.

NATHANIEL HAWTHORNE

The golden opportunity you are seeking is in yourself. It is not in your environment; it is not in luck or chance, or the help of others; it is in yourself alone.

ORISON SWETT MARDEN

Too many people overvalue what they are not and undervalue what they are.

MALCOLM FORBES

Life is not the way it's supposed to be. It's the way it is. The way you cope with it is what makes the difference.

VIRGINIA SATIR

When one door closes, another door opens; but we often look so long and regretfully upon the closed door that we do not see the ones which open.

ALEXANDER GRAHAM BELL

The truth is incontrovertible. Malice may attack it and ignorance may deride it, but in the end, there it is.

WINSTON CHURCHILL

The great enemy of the truth is very often not the lie— deliberate, contrived and dishonest; but the myth— persistent, persuasive and unrealistic.

JOHN F. KENNEDY

Monday Morning Choice #12

The Legacy Choice . . .
Give Your Gift

In everyone's life, at some time, our inner fire goes out.
It is then burst into flame by an encounter with another human being.
We should all be thankful for those people who rekindle the inner spirit.
ALBERT SCHWEITZER

Jim Spier has been giving of himself through the Boy
Scouts for many years. Drawing from personal experience,
he provides this interesting insight:

In your mind's eye, take a look at any 100 boys who
have recently joined Scouting:

- Of those 100 boys, rarely will one ever appear before a juvenile court.

- Twelve of the 100 will receive their first religious contact through Scouting.

- Eighteen will develop hobbies and interests that will last all their lives.

- Eight will find their future vocation through badge work and Scouting contacts.

- One will use Scouting skills to save another person's life, and one will be credited with saving his own life.

- Seventeen will become future Scout leaders and will give leadership to additional thousands of boys.

For the sake of comparison, according to the Justice Department's Report on Juvenile Crime (Washington, D.C., U.S. Government Printing Office, 2002), there were 2.3 million juvenile arrests in the United States in 2001.

Of that group, 1,400 were arrested for murder. Approximately 500,000 arrests were made for burglary, theft, auto theft, and arson. More than 105,000 youth were arrested for vandalism, 37,500 were arrested for carrying weapons, and 202,500 were arrested on illegal drug charges.

What is the difference between the Scouts and the arrested juveniles?

Of course, many factors could come into play, but one obvious difference is that the Scouts have someone guiding them—a mentor who provides light through the pitch-black darkness of making choices.

The choice of legacy, whether as a Boy or Girl Scout leader, a business mentor, a teacher, or a volunteer consultant, is an important choice, and a necessary choice for you to achieve success.

Moreover, without people choosing the legacy choice, our society would be stymied. There would be no positive role models, examples, endowments, helping hands, help for the homeless, or voice for the voiceless.

Think back to your own childhood. Without too much effort, not only can you probably name an adult mentor, outside your family, who left an imprint on your life, but also you can probably envision that person's face or a specific activity.

In most cases, these important individuals were passionate about their mission, whether it was showing you the ropes in your first job or showing you how to dribble a basketball in elementary school. They not only knew the importance of giving of themselves but also saw you as an important recipient of their gifts.

Getting the Cold Hard—
and Valuable—Facts

When I first began my business, I went to visit Fred Smith, an author and a mentor to many successful businesspeople in Dallas. He is one of the wisest men I've ever met. But his approach to mentoring sessions was far from coddling me, the neophyte.

Instead, he was brutal with me as he provided information that was honest and that I value, even today, as some of the most important information I would hear. He painted no pretty pictures, served up no pie in the sky. Instead, he immediately seized my attention and told me not only how it was going to be but how to avoid certain unavoidable obstacles in the future.

The times I spent with Fred Smith provided me with more information and more momentum than any college degree or any experience in the field.

More than once, in my own presentations and in my books, I have referred to Fred's guidance. It is his legacy that I value more than words can express.

But what would happen if there were no willing mentors like Fred Smith or Jim Spier?

Without mentors, we would not have the wealth of past experience to call upon, or the wisdom to look beyond the horizon for the next strategy or direction. Without willing volunteers, how many thousands of children and young adults would go without exposure to quality experiences and individuals with something to share?

Many successful men and women hold in common the choice to leave behind a legacy that will live on long after their last breaths.

After all is said and done, are we here to give a bit of ourselves to others? Aren't we ultimately defined and remembered by what we give?

Why should we choose to give?

It takes a lot of endurance to put other people first, particularly when they're often so preoccupied with themselves that they don't seem to notice our efforts. Furthermore, our schedules are normally full, even before we start giving our time and energy to others.

But we should choose to give because it is the right thing to do.

People and Peanuts

George Washington Carver not only knew something about peanuts but also was intimately familiar with the human condition. He understood the importance of legacy, of giving to others, when he said, "How far you go in life depends on your being tender with the young, compassionate with the aged, sympathetic with the striving, and tolerant of the weak and the strong . . . because someday in life you will have been all of these."

When asked about giving of ourselves, another wise sage counseled, "Don't expect the people you help to be there to help you when you're in need yourself."

Excellent advice! The purpose of giving is not to receive back in full measure. If you give solely with the expectation of receiving something in return, prepare to be disappointed. After all, if expecting something in return is your reason for giving, you are really not giving but swapping. If you receive something in return for your gift, what you receive is a bonus, not a repayment of debt.

When you put someone else first, your gift smoothes off the rough edges that makes human relationships difficult. You're rounding off the corners that have prevented the square pegs from fitting into society's round holes. But don't expect a thank-you note or a pat on the head. Choose to give because it is the right thing to do.

Begin Your Legacy Where You Are

Some attempt to sidestep giving of themselves by saying, "I wouldn't know where to start or what to give."

Giving back can be as simple as working overtime so another employee can attend her daughter's soccer game. It can be answering the phones during a telethon or speaking to a group of students on career day. Only your time and wisdom are required to build a legacy.

The ancient Roman philosopher Seneca anticipated this hesitancy about knowing where to start. "Where there is another human being," he wrote, "there is always an opportunity for kindness."

Start with the person who sits next to you at work—your peer, your boss, or just an acquaintance. Start somewhere. You never know where you will make the difference that will change a person's life.

The Unreachable Student

At the end of the semester, a college professor was looking over her students as they took the final examination. Her eyes encountered one student, a young woman, who seemed too absorbed in things outside the classroom to ever make much of a contribution. The professor shook her head, feeling as though she had not done enough to reach the girl. It was rare she did not connect with her students. This student seemed to be disinterested and just going through the motions.

At the end of the final examination, the young woman placed her exam on the professor's desk and handed her an envelope. On its front, the student had taped two candy canes. Inside was a holiday card with the usual message—but beneath the printed message, the student had written the following:

> *Thank you for making me feel—for the first time—that my ideas were important and that I had something of value, something to contribute to your class. I will never forget you.*

Don't judge the impact of your legacy solely on the outward response of those around you. Many times, when we are least aware of it, a gesture, an encouraging word, or a smile will encourage others more than we'll ever know.

The Law of Legacy

Giving of ourselves should come from the heart and, without fail, when this kind of giving happens, we are generously repaid for every kindness we share.

September 13, 2000, was a defining day in my life. On the previous day, my wife Karen had been sent by her doctor for a biopsy. I thought—and she thought—it was just an infection, but when I answered the phone, our worst fears were realized. Karen had a very rare form of cancer.

Within 24 hours, she had begun chemotherapy and we were approaching a period in our lives no one wants to think about, much less experience.

Before that day and for the 22 years of our marriage, Karen had always been "the giver" in our family. Anytime someone had a need, Karen was the first person there, always willing to help, never asking for anything in return.

On September 14, when others began hearing about her situation, we were bombarded by people wanting to help. Some were strangers to us. As a teacher, Karen had helped their children. For several months—not weeks but months—after she began fighting this case of aggressive cancer, people were cleaning our house, bringing meals, taking care of all our needs to allow us to focus every ounce of our energies in the fight against this devastating and often fatal disease.

The people who gave of themselves and their time to help us stepped up because Karen had always been a giver. Now she had given them the best gift of all—an opportunity to give back.

What we do for others eventually comes back to us, multiplied . . . maybe not from those we help or even from the people we know. I have seen it happen many times and have been a recipient of its rich rewards. It is the law of legacy.

Trusted Mentors Leave Their Marks

Most successful people have the luxury of a mentor. Maybe for you it was a grandparent, a teacher, or a colleague. Someone was there to provide sound advice while you were blazing a career or personal path foreign to you. That mentor was able to clear the fog from your vision.

For Mitch Albom, a terrific writer, his mentor was Morrie Schwartz, his college professor. For twenty years or so, Mitch lost track of Morrie, as his career was consuming all of his time and energy.

Mitch rediscovered Morrie in Morrie's last months of life. Knowing that Morrie was dying, Mitch began meeting with him every Tuesday, and Morrie shared his life lessons with Mitch. The result was a wonderful book, *Tuesdays with Morrie*.

Morrie left a lasting legacy through his time with Mitch, and Mitch's gift and legacy were writing *Tuesdays with Morrie*, which allows all of us to learn from a wise mentor.

I never met Morrie or Mitch, but their legacy continues to live through me. *Tuesdays with Morrie* was my inspiration to write *Monday Morning Mentoring*, which has had an impact on hundreds of thousands of other people.

You never know how your legacy will continue to grow.

Mentoring—Sharing the Way Out

Once a man was walking down the street and fell into a hole. The hole was so deep he could not escape. He looked in all directions and could not figure out how to raise himself from the hole.

A preacher walked by, heard the man's cry for help, and inquired, "Why are you in that hole in the road?" The man replied, "I fell in and I can't get out." The preacher said that he would pray for him and walked away.

A police officer walked by, heard the man's cry for help, and inquired, "Why are you in that hole in the road?" The man replied, "I fell in and I can't get out." The policeman said it was against the law to be in a hole in the road, wrote him a ticket, threw it into the hole, and walked away.

An environmentalist walked by, heard the man's cry for help, and inquired, "Why are you in that hole in the road?" The man replied, "I fell in and I can't get out." The environmentalist said it was environmentally unsafe to be in a hole in the road and began to picket, circling the hole and holding a sign reading, "Man in Hole in Road . . . Environmentally Unsafe!"

A friend walked by, heard the man's cry for help, and inquired, "Why are you in that hole in the road?" The man replied, "I fell in and I can't get out." Without hesitation, the friend jumped into the hole with him.

The man in the hole said, "Are you crazy? Why did you jump in this hole? I have tried my best, but I cannot find a way out. I have had preachers praying for me, police writing me a ticket, and this goofy person picketing outside . . . and you chose to jump down here with me. Are you crazy? Why would you jump down here with me?"

The friend replied, "Don't worry. I chose to jump in this

hole with you because I have been in this hole before, and I know the way out!"

Maybe you have not faced a situation that led to being in a "deep hole." Nevertheless, you can listen to, coach, and support those who are working their way out of the holes they have fallen into.

Trusted counselors, mentors, and guides make an indelible mark on the lives they touch, and they provide the two ingredients to success in life—caring and sharing—that cannot be learned or purchased. There is no scarcity of people who could use your experience and guidance to make better choices in their lives.

What is your legacy? What marks are you leaving along the path for the next generation?

We leave our legacies by choice. No one requires us to make this contribution. We do this to help someone along the way—to support our colleagues, our friends, and those whom we may not know. It is a gift that comes without a price tag. Your legacy is priceless.

You may be successful, but your choice to leave a legacy by giving of yourself distinguishes you most, providing the greatest meaning to your life. Your example will live into the next generation through the lives you touch.

The bottom line is that whatever you have learned, whatever you possess, is not yours to keep. It is yours to pass on.

Three Things You Can Do to Make the Legacy Choice

1. Be willing to share what you know and to mentor those looking for the pathway to success.

2. The greatest gift you can give is your knowledge and experiences. Giving of yourself should come from the heart, and when this kind of giving happens, you are generously repaid for every kindness you share.

3. Begin your legacy where you are—there's always an opportunity for others to learn from you.

Monday Morning Discussion Questions

1. Think about those who have shared their legacies with you: a relative, a coach, a professor, or your current boss. Discuss how this has made a difference in your life.

2. What specific legacy do you think you can offer to another?

3. Think of opportunities for your team to provide a helping hand to someone in need of help—in your office or your community.

Words of Wisdom about the
Legacy Choice

In this world it is not what we take up, but what we give up, that makes us rich.

HENRY WARD BEECHER

It is one of the most beautiful compensations of life, that no man can sincerely try to help another without helping himself.

RALPH WALDO EMERSON

When you share, the remainder multiplies and grows.

W. CLEMENT STONE

The best thing about giving of ourselves is that what we get is always better than what we give. The reaction is greater than the action.

ORISON SWETT MARDEN

If you can't feed a hundred people, then feed just one.

MOTHER TERESA

We make a living from what we get; we make a life from what we give.

WINSTON CHURCHILL

Generous people are rarely mentally ill people.

DR. KARL MENNINGER

I don't know what your destiny will be, but one thing I do know: the only ones among you who will be really happy are those who have sought and found how to serve.

ALBERT SCHWEITZER

Sharing makes you bigger than you are. The more you pour out, the more life will be able to pour in.

JIM ROHN

When you were born, you cried and the world rejoiced. Live your life in such a manner that when you die the world cries and you rejoice.

OLD INDIAN SAYING

There are two ways of spreading light: to be the candle or the mirror that reflects it.

EDITH WHARTON

Plant a kernel of wheat and you reap a pint; plant a pint and you reap a bushel. Always the law works to give you back more than you give.

ANTHONY NORVELL

Sharing what you have is more important than what you have.

ALBERT M. WELLS, JR.

Give and it shall be given to you. A good measure, pressed down, shaken together, and running over, will be poured into your lap. For with the measure you use, it will be measured to you.

LUKE 6:38 (NIV)

You only get to keep what you give away.

SHELDON KOPP

Preparing for Your Special Moment of Success

To every man there comes in his lifetime that special moment when he is tapped on the shoulder and offered the chance to do a special thing unique to him and fitted to his talents. What a tragedy if that moment finds him unprepared or unqualified for the work which would be his finest hour.
WINSTON CHURCHILL

This book was written to help you prepare for your special moment of success.

Andrew Carnegie once said, "The average person puts only 25 percent of his energy and ability into his work. The world takes off its hat to those who put in more than 50 percent of their capacity and stands on its head for those few and far between souls who devote 100 percent."

What a shame!

Becoming successful is hard work, and, like a business, it must be budgeted. The business budget is the plan for expenditures, appropriate allocation of resources, and accounting of results. The budget must be somewhat fluid, as adjustments have to be made to account for changing conditions.

Planning your career success is the same. Plan where you will expend your time and energy, focus on the important activities that help you accomplish your plan, and hold yourself accountable for success.

There is a price to be paid for success, but I have discovered that most successful people do not consider the price as a cost or fee. The top people in their field enjoy their careers and the work involved, and they enjoy the journey.

Payne Stewart won the U.S. Open in 1999. Shortly after that victory, he perished in a tragic airplane accident. Payne was a charismatic, fun-loving person who had a passion for his work combined with a deep faith in his purpose. Shortly before his death, he was quoted thus: "The thing about dreams is sometimes you get to live them out."

That is how I feel about my career: I am getting to live out my dreams! My dream is to encourage others to become the very best in whatever role they have chosen in life. That is the purpose of *Monday Morning Choices*.

The choices you make will determine whether you get to live out your dreams. Your success increases or decreases in value every day on the basis of your choices. Most of the time, it is not just one choice that separates the successful from those who fall short of success. It is an accumulation of many choices that make the difference.

You have far too much talent to be average. I hope you will make the choice to be one of the few-and-far-between souls who give everything they have to become successful. Our world needs more opportunities to stand on its head!

My desire is that the information in this book will motivate you to make the choices you need to become the very best at your chosen profession. Make the choice to do something, and go as far as you can see. When you get there, you will know where to go next.

May life's journey bring you good choices, success, and prosperity!

12 Choices—12 Questions

The Character Choices

1. The no-victim choice—don't let your past eat your future.

Do I accept total responsibility for my success?

2. The commitment choice—be passionate enough to succeed.

Am I committed to paying the price of success?

3. The values choice—choose the right enemies.

Do I accept that there will be enemies who oppose my values?

4. The integrity choice—do the right thing.

Will my success be accomplished without a sacrifice of my integrity?

The Action Choices

5. The do-something choice—don't vacation on Someday Isle.

Will I attack complacency and do something daily toward success?

6. The persistence choice—learn from failure.

Will I hang in there, beyond failure, long enough to achieve success?

7. The attitude choice—take the enthusiastic approach.
Will I take a positive approach to the unexpected twists and turns of life?

8. The adversity choice—conquer difficult times.
Will I attack adversity, regardless of what happens along the way?

The Investment Choices
9. The relationship choice—connect with success.
Will I invest time in building positive relationships?

10. The criticism choice—embrace tough learning.
Do I accept criticism as valuable feedback?

11. The reality choice—face the truth.
Am I true to myself and all those around me?

12. The legacy choice—give your gift.
Do I share the gift of my experience and knowledge with others?

The Final Question
Am I prepared for my special moment of success?
12 Choices—12 Questions Reminder Card
(laminated card) is available at
www.CornerStoneLeadership.com

Five Ways to Bring *Monday Morning Choices* into Your Organization:

1. *Monday Morning Choices* PowerPoint Presentation

Introduce and reinforce the *Monday Morning Choices* to your organization with this complete and cost-effective presentation. All the main concepts and ideas in the book are reinforced in this professionally produced, downloadable PowerPoint presentation with facilitator guide and notes. Available at www.CornerStoneLeadership.com for $99.95.

2. Keynote Presentation

Invite author David Cottrell to inspire your team and help create greater success for your organization. Each presentation is designed to set a solid foundation for both organizational and personal success. Contact Michele Lucia at (972) 899-3411 or at Michele@CornerStoneLeadership.com.

3. *Monday Morning Choices* Workshop

Facilitated by David Cottrell or a certified CornerStone Leadership instructor, this three-hour or six-hour workshop will reinforce the principles of *Monday Morning Choices*. Each participant will develop a personal action plan that can make a profound difference in his or her life and career.

4. *Monday Morning Choices* Profile

This online profile assesses your personal strengths and provides insight into gaps that may be preventing your success. It provides the framework for the creation of an actionable development plan that leverages the concepts of *Monday Morning Choices*. Available at www.CornerStoneLeadership.com for $19.95.

5. *Monday Morning Choices* Audio CD

Available at www.CornerStoneLeadership.com or call 888–789-LEAD (5323). $19.95.

Free downloadable *Monday Morning Choices* workbook available at www.CornerStoneLeadership.com.

Acknowledgments

O ver the years, I have been one of the most fortunate people in the world because of my family, friends, and associates. My success has been molded and formed by those with whom I have been fortunate enough to be on the same team.

Thanks to my family, who have been my inspiration:

My wife, Karen, who made the adversity choice to fight and win her battle against cancer. She is now a positive role model for many others who are facing the battle for their lives.

My daughter Jennifer, who made the choice to persist and work her way through the traps into which so many young adults fall victim.

My daughter Kim, who made the choice of doing something and becoming the most supportive, positive, and loving daughter anyone could ask for.

And my son, Michael, who made the attitude choice of

living his life in a positive, enthusiastic manner, regardless of any challenge he may face.

Thanks to my friends who have been my encouragement: Ty Deleon, Logan Garrett, Eric Harvey, Louis Kruger, Mark Layton, Bryan Lancaster, Joe Miles, Tod Taylor, and many others who have helped me through the good times and the times when adversity seemed overwhelming.

Thanks to the CornerStone team that has been the reason for my success: Barbara Bartlett, Ken Carnes, Lee Colan, Jim Garner, Harry Hopkins, Shawn Kirwan, Suzanne McClelland, and Melissa Monogue.

And especially Alice Adams, who made her legacy choice eight years ago by mentoring me and providing me with her knowledge and expertise on how to write books.

Thanks to David Hale Smith, my literary agent, and the HarperCollins team of Sarah Brown, Angie Lee, Larry Hughes, Margot Schupf, and Ethan Friedman for bringing *Monday Morning Choices* to life.

To each person who reads this book, best wishes as you make the right choices to accomplish the success you deserve.

About the Author

David Cottrell, president and CEO of CornerStone Leadership Institute, is an internationally known leadership consultant, educator, and speaker. His business experience includes leadership positions with Xerox and FedEx. He also led the successful turnaround of a Chapter 11 company before founding CornerStone.

He is the author of more than twenty books, including *Monday Morning Mentoring; Listen Up, Leader; The Next Level: Leadership Beyond the Status Quo; Monday Morning Leadership; Leadership . . . Biblically Speaking; Management Insights; Leadership Courage;* and *Birdies, Pars, and Bogeys: Leadership Lessons from the Links.*

David is a thought-provoking and electrifying professional speaker. He has presented his leadership message to over 250,000 managers worldwide. His powerful wisdom and insights on leadership have made him a highly sought after keynote speaker and seminar leader.

He and his wife, Karen, reside in Horseshoe Bay, Texas. David can be reached at www.CornerStoneLeadership.com.